1974

Swiss Drawings

Swiss Drawings

MASTERPIECES OF FIVE CENTURIES

Introduction and Notes by Walter Hugelshofer

Organized by the Pro Helvetia Foundation

Smithsonian Institution Press

Washington, D. C.

1967

*The material for this work was prepared under the direction of the Pro Helvetia Foundation.
It is available in a softcover catalog of the Swiss Drawings exhibition circulated by the
Smithsonian Institution Traveling Exhibition Service to the following:*

National Gallery of Art WASHINGTON, D. C.
The Pierpont Morgan Library NEW YORK, NEW YORK
M. H. de Young Memorial Museum SAN FRANCISCO, CALIFORNIA
The Art Institute of Chicago CHICAGO, ILLINOIS

SMITHSONIAN PUBLICATION 4716   DESIGNED BY CRIMILDA PONTES
PRODUCED BY THE MERIDEN GRAVURE COMPANY AND THE ANTHOENSEN PRESS
LIBRARY OF CONGRESS CATALOG CARD NUMBER 67-28923

Acknowledgments

Swiss Drawings–Masterpieces of Five Centuries is the first exhibition of its kind to be brought to this country. It marks the first time that the American museum visitor has had the privilege of viewing the full sweep of Swiss draftsmanship from the sixteenth to the present century, from Holbein to Giacometti.

The exhibition has become a reality chiefly through the good will of the many lenders, both public and private, who have graciously consented to part with their treasures for a long period. It is their generosity which has enabled us to bring such a superb collection to the United States.

To the Pro Helvetia Foundation must go our profound thanks. From its inception the project has been guided and directed with the greatest care and attention by Mr. Luc Boissonnas, Secretary General of the Foundation, and his entire staff, especially Mrs. H. Wüthrich, secretary. Thanks to the generous support of the Foundation, we were able to include a number of particularly fine works which otherwise might not have been part of the exhibition. With consummate skill and patience, Mr. Walter Hugelshofer and the Pro Helvetia Foundation performed the complex undertaking of assembling the drawings in Switzerland and attending to the myriad details involved in bringing the collection to this country. Our sincere thanks are due also to Mr. Hugelshofer for the dual tasks of making the selection of the drawings and writing the introduction and catalog notes. Mr. Hugelshofer's work was made possible through the generosity of the Pro Helvetia Foundation. A word of thanks, too, must go to Dr. Hanspeter Landolt for his early work on and encouragement of the project.

His Excellency, Felix Schnyder, the Ambassador of Switzerland, has graciously agreed to sponsor the exhibition while it is on tour in the United States. We are most grateful to Mr. Lukas Burckhardt, Counselor for Cultural Affairs of the Embassy of Switzerland, for his constant help and encouragement during all stages of the negotiations.

Our gratitude is extended to Dr. and Mrs. Edgar Breitenbach for their skillful translation of the German text of the catalog, and to Mrs. Emily Evershed for her work in editing the text. The coordination of all the many intricate matters of negotiation, transport, preparation, and publication of the catalog were handled by Miss Frances P. Smyth of the staff of the Traveling Exhibition Service, an office of the United States National Museum, under the direction of Mrs. Dorothy T. Van Arsdale.

S. DILLON RIPLEY, *Secretary*
Smithsonian Institution

The Pro Helvetia Foundation

Located in Zurich, the Pro Helvetia Foundation for Cultural Relations with Foreign Countries was originally created in 1939 both to maintain and promote Switzerland's spiritual and cultural heritage and to foster appreciation of the works and achievements of Swiss thought and culture in other countries. The organization assumed its present form in 1949. It is a public foundation under the supervision of the Swiss Federal Council. In addition to sending printed materials abroad, it organizes exhibitions, concerts and lectures in foreign countries. The Foundation also receives distinguished foreign visitors who come to Switzerland to study some aspect of the life of the country. Pro Helvetia's constant endeavor is to present other countries with the highest expression of Swiss cultural life.

Lenders to the Exhibition

The Federal Gottfried Keller Foundation

Arlesheim, Professor Arthur Stoll

Basel, Dr. Paul Hänggi

Basel, Oeffentliche Kunstsammlung,
Print Room

Basel, Dr. and Mrs. Franz Meyer

Basel, Dr. Willi Raeber

Berlin, Staatliche Museen, Print Room,
Stiftung Preussischer Kulturbesitz

Bern, Historisches Museum

Bern, Mr. E. W. Kornfeld

Bern, Kunstmuseum

Darmstadt, Hessisches Landesmuseum

Diessenhofen, Mr. Carl Roesch

Donaueschingen, Fürstlich-
Fürstenbergische Collection

Geneva, Musée d'Art et d'Histoire

Geneva, Mr. Janos Scholz

Karlsruhe, Staatliche Kunsthalle

La Tour de Peilz, Miss Claire Oederlin

Lausanne, Mr. Claude Vallotton

Lausanne, Mr. Maxime Vallotton

Lucerne, Kunstmuseum

Montreux, Dr. Gabathuler

Munich, Graphische Sammlung

Nuremberg, Germanisches Nationalmuseum

Winterthur, Mr. Willi Dünner

Winterthur, Kunstmuseum

Winterthur, Dr. A. Werner

Zofingen, Stadtbibliothek

Zurich, Mrs. Nelly Bär

Zurich, Eidgenössische Technische
Hochschule, Print Collection

Zurich, Kunsthaus

Zurich, Schweizerisches Landesmuseum

85. WOLFGANG TÖPFFER, *Picnic beside Lake Leman*

Introduction

It is interesting to speculate why art of a high quality makes its first appearance in a particular country. In the case of Switzerland, the great moment resulted from a series of unexpected and extraordinary events. In 1476-77 the Swiss peasant army vanquished the Duke of Burgundy, Charles the Bold, after his invasion. Charles was the richest and most powerful ruler of his time, and his defeat had repercussions throughout the whole of Europe. In 1499 the Swiss defeated the German Emperor Maximilian I and secured their independence from the Holy Roman Empire. They next intervened in the struggle between the Hapsburgs and France for the possession of Lombardy and other parts of Italy, and again were victorious in several major battles. Waging war came to be regarded as a means of overcoming the endemic poverty which the Swiss had long accepted as a way of life, and the victorious soldier, with his display of booty, became the hero archetype.

Confidence gained through military successes, horizons widened by discovery of the New World, and a new religious ferment all helped to shape the talent of two remarkable artists, Niklaus Manuel in Bern and Urs Graf in Basel. Both were essentially draftsmen, and both were fascinated by the mercenaries. Despite a similarity in the subject of their work, each shows a marked difference in treatment. Manuel—highly sensitive, intellectually inquisitive, and given to philosophic reflection—was in certain respects remote from the everyday world. He viewed the wars, with their deadly man-to-man combat, in a romantic light, and concentrated on the splendid costume in which the mercenary paraded at home. By choice he ignored

9

the tragic and negative side of war and actually gained pleasure from its various manifestations. His style may have been influenced by certain chiaroscuro drawings of Hans Baldung. When, in 1522, he had the option of giving up painting in exchange for a position as provincial governor, he seems to have found no difficulty in making the transition. He was not satisfied by his success, and it may be that he felt his creative powers were diminishing. Manuel drew only occasionally in his later years, and died at the age of forty-five.

Manuel's contemporary, the goldsmith Urs Graf of Basel, had an entirely different temperament. He actually participated in and enjoyed the rough life of the mercenaries. An acute observer, he was endowed with the faculty of self-criticism and with a grim sense of humor. He was keenly aware of the negative side of war and did not hesitate to record it. His drawings emphasize the horror of battle: the soldier returning home empty-handed, the girl he had left behind, and a man dangling from the gallows. Urs Graf drew these scenes knowing full well that he himself might one day meet a similar fate. His drawings—highly personal documents—were never commissioned, nor, indeed, were they ever meant to be sold, and they were probably fully appreciated only by his fellow mercenaries. Frequently they are startlingly savage and brutal in style and subject matter; in some of them, Graf approached true genius. Like Manuel, he was active as an artist for scarcely more than a dozen years, and his last drawings lack the brilliance of his earlier work.

Hans Leu, a contemporary of Manuel and Graf, and the son of a painter, was active mainly in Zurich. His training brought him to Nuremberg, however, about 1510, where he studied with Dürer, whose work was then widely influential. Leu was admitted to Dürer's workshop and through it he became acquainted with the work of Hans Baldung in Strasbourg. In 1513 Leu returned to Zurich, where he took over his father's workshop. He painted altarpieces and murals and made designs for the glass painters. As a citizen, he was obliged to participate in military campaigns but was evidently so little enamoured of these experiences that he never sketched a single mercenary. When Dürer came to Zurich in 1519 (accompanied by Pirckheimer and Martin Tucher) he visited his former pupil, and in 1523 he sent Leu his greetings in a letter.

The work of Hans Leu reveals a gentle disposition and the sensitive, imaginative mind of a poet. His strongest and most original work deals with nature. Leu was one of the first artists to portray the beauty of windswept trees and distant snow-covered mountains. He took an active part in the Reformation and was killed while fighting at the side of the reformer, Ulrich Zwingli.

The visual arts flourished in Basel at the beginning of the sixteenth century. As in any period of intellectual curiosity, the interest in books was great. Artists could count on a steady flow of commissions from book publishers, who were filling a current demand for designs for pictorial title pages and text illustrations, to be reproduced in woodblocks.

In addition to Urs Graf, the talented Master D. S., possibly a Netherlandish artist, was also active in Basel. For a brief period in the course of his travels, the young Dürer visited Basel, where the brothers Ambrosius and Hans Holbein the Younger, had also settled after leaving Augsburg. Both made many drawings for Basel publishers. While untimely death cut short Ambrosius' career (about 1519), Hans developed rapidly as an artist, becoming a master of unusual stature, and his work exerted a far-reaching influence on subsequent artists. In addition to his work on book illustrations, Holbein made many drawings for window designs, to be executed by glass painters. Some were commissioned, while others were done on speculation, as seen in his blank escutcheons intended for armorial bearings. The glass painter would adapt such drawings to his own medium. Making gifts of skillfully painted windows was a popular Swiss custom of the time. In part done for aesthetic enjoyment, there was also prestige attached to such a donation. A coat of arms and a tablet bearing the name of the donor and the date of the gift was inscribed on the lower portion of the window, and the picture itself frequently contained an allusion to the occupation of the person for whom it was intended, or to some important event in his life. In the upper part there was usually an illustration of some contemporary pastime, such as hunting or target practice. Holbein used this traditional scheme quite freely and varied it by introducing spatial elements, thereby giving a new direction to this type of glass painting.

The painting of building façades with architecture seen in perspective was then fashionable, and the roots of this practice can be traced back to Italy and even to antiquity. (It was, however, unsuited to the damp climate of the northern countries, and most of these paintings have been lost through deterioration.) The often asymmetrical façades of Gothic buildings were transformed almost beyond recognition by painted architectural elements—such as colonnades and arcades—in the classical style of the Renaissance. Holbein's painting in this new field had a quality of opulence, in contrast to the narrower and more pedantic work of local artists.

Hans Holbein the Younger was born in Augsburg at the end of the fifteenth century. He matured at a time when the new ideas of Renaissance art were filtering through to the countries north of the Alps and replacing the traditional Gothic forms. In his father's workshop he saw portraits (some painted, but the majority drawn) with a new concept of man's relation to the world. Because he grew up with these new ideas, Hans the Younger was never a Gothic artist. He did not have to struggle to absorb and master the new forms.

As an objective artist rather than an emotional and expressive one, Holbein seems to have created with relative ease. His pen stroke is strong and assured, and his lines are even and relaxed. He indicates shadows by applying washes with his brush, mostly in gray tones, which gives his drawings a softened, painterly character. His works are emphatically three-dimensional. These techniques and others were acquired from Hans the Elder, who had probably learned them in the Low Countries. In their use of washes for modeling, the Holbeins differed from other Germanic draftsmen, who indicated shadows by crosshatching with a pen, a technique which gave to their work an expressive, restless element.

Early in his career Hans Holbein the Younger became a painter of altarpieces for churches in Basel, a most important source of income for artists. No preliminary sketches for these altarpieces exist, possibly because Holbein never saw the need of making any. There are, however, drawings for the portraits of the donors, which appeared on these panels. Holbein sketched his sitters from life, and he painted the portraits from these sketches. This he did in order to save his usually rich and aristocratic sitters the burden of repeated visits to his studio. The social gulf between artist and patron was considerable at the time, even when the artist was of the highest rank. As Holbein observed these social differences throughout his career, his portrait painting taught him to rely heavily on both his memory and his great skill.

By 1524 Holbein was a member of the painters' guild with citizenship in Basel. He had married a local woman by whom he had two sons, had worked for the mayor and other high-ranking patrons, and had been commissioned by the city council to paint murals in the council chamber of the town hall. Despite all this activity, he seems to have become restless in Basel. There were signs, too, of religious turmoil and social upheaval in Basel which probably affected him. In any event, the future seemed uncertain.

In 1524 Holbein traveled to France, to try for the position of court painter, now that Leonardo da Vinci was dead. Nothing came of this, as the young artist was not yet sufficiently well known. In 1526, through the good offices of Erasmus, Holbein managed to gain a foothold in London. There he acquired some recognition as a portrait painter among the humanists and scholars, but their financial means were limited. Two years later he returned to Basel to see his family. He bought a house and made an attempt to settle down again, but the advent of the Reformation, preceded by riots and followed by the ban on art in the churches, destroyed the basis of his livelihood. It was a difficult and frustrating time for an established painter. The city of Basel tried to hold him with an offer of a pension and of a further commission in the town hall, but Holbein felt that there was far too little potential for him in Basel. He went back to London in 1532, again leaving his family behind, and this time success came his way. A number of German merchants in London, who had formed a guild, had him paint their portraits; he also decorated their guildhall with murals. His reputation grew. The two French ambassadors to the Court of St. James sat for Holbein, and his double portrait of them is a masterpiece. From that time commissions came easily. Even Henry VIII, who had just brought the Reformation to England, had his portrait painted by Holbein, and the King's favorites followed suit. When Holbein was commissioned to do murals for Whitehall Palace, his fame spread. Unable to handle the volume of work by himself, he hired assistants. Like Jan van Eyck before him and Rubens after him, Holbein was sent out by the court to paint portraits. Whether this also involved confidential missions, we do not know. When, on one of these occasions, he visited Basel again, he was received with great honors. The visit served to convince him that he had outgrown the narrow world of his earlier years. A permanent return to Basel was out of the question. Nor was it feasible to remove his family to England to settle in alien surroundings. Thus Holbein lived alone in London from 1532 until his death in 1543. His circle there consisted of fellow artists, goldsmiths, miniaturists, and engravers.

From 1532 on, Holbein's output consisted only of portraits and of designs for goldsmiths, enamelers, and embroiderers. During this time he produced only one picture with a religious theme. The splendor of the English court, his travels, and his contacts with other artists and their work all affected Holbein's art and his view of the world considerably. His outlook became freer and his detachment more pronounced. In the sketches he made as designs for paintings, engravings, and other arts, one can see that the late Gothic world was far behind him.

His studies in colored chalks, made from life and subsequently used for his portrait paintings, constitute an impressive body of work. They possess a natural grandeur and dignity of a kind hitherto unknown in art. Curiously, these portraits were working drawings and not intended to be regarded as works of art in themselves. They have been preserved, with a few exceptions, and today are found in Windsor Castle and in the Basel Museum.

The advent of the Reformation, and a resultant hostility toward religious art, had profound repercussions on the intellectual life of the Western world. For centuries the Church had nurtured art, and with it, the artists themselves. The commissions of lay patrons, now the chief source of income, could not compare favorably with those of the Church. Art was relegated to a much lower status, and the Germanic countries entered a period of gradual artistic decline. Some artists adhered to the old religion and moved to find work in Catholic regions, while others earned their livelihood as painters of portraits or of heraldic designs. Tobias Stimmer (1539-1584), the greatest Swiss painter of the generation after Holbein, decorated façades of houses, made designs for woodcuts and windows, and excelled as a portraitist. He worked in the scholarly, classical manner introduced by Holbein. His pupil Lindtmeyer (1552-1604), despite considerable talent, found it difficult to make a living as a designer of windows. Religious and social tensions, at times leading to open warfare, continued to paralyze the creative spirit. By the close of the sixteenth century, significant artistic activity had come to a virtual standstill in Switzerland. Although art flourished in the Netherlands, Spain, Italy, and France during the seventeenth century, this was a barren period in both Switzerland and Germany.

In the eighteenth century the Swiss traveling artist made his appearance. Such a man, after modest training at home, went abroad to acquire more experience and often made his reputation outside of Switzerland. An example is Freudenberger (1745-1801) from Bern, who worked in Paris at the time of Boucher and Greuze and who became an important book illustrator. Other Swiss artists who worked abroad include: Anton Graff (1736-1813), a leading portrait painter in Dresden; Joseph Werner (1637-1710) from Bern, who headed Berlin's new Academy (modeled on the French Academy); the bizarre Johann Heinrich Füssli (1741-1825), who often took his subject matter from literature and who became famous in London as John Henry Fuseli. There was also the painter Jean Étienne Liotard (1702-1789) from Geneva, who enjoyed the highest reputation, and whose pastel portraits were in great demand throughout Europe.

Inspired by the writings of Rousseau, about the middle of the eighteenth century a new preoccupation with nature made itself felt. The artist's attitude toward nature changed, and a new approach became evident. For Caspar Wolff (1735-1783) the Alps, which for centuries had seemed barren and forbidding to the beholder, became a source of inspiration, overwhelming in their majesty. Ludwig Aberli (1723-1786) had an eye for the serene loveliness of the surrounding countryside. He delighted in the beauty of the Swiss lakes and was fascinated by medieval ruins—in direct opposition to sophisticated European taste of that time. After Aberli came a number of minor artists—such as Rieter, Biedermann (1763-1830), König, and Lory

—whose color engravings of landscapes and costumes satisfied the demand for souvenirs on the part of foreign tourists, many of whom came to view the newly discovered scenic attractions of the Alps.

At this time art began to flourish in the French-speaking cantons, and especially in Geneva, where artists were encouraged by Liotard's success. A group of these painters—among them Saint-Ours, De La Rive, Agasse, Massot, and Töpffer (1766-1847)—captured the beauty and the poetry of the Swiss countryside and the contented lives of its inhabitants.

By the nineteenth century Switzerland began to develop a cultural identity, no easy matter for a country that had originated as a voluntary, loose confederation of cantons which were largely autonomous and free to maintain their distinct cultural heritages. The cantons belong linguistically to three large groups—the Germans, French, and Italians—and became united politically, but their cultural ties have been with the much larger neighboring countries with which they share a common language. For this reason there is no Swiss art in the sense that there is a Dutch art, for example.

At the beginning of the twentieth century, modern art came to Switzerland through the influence of Ferdinand Hodler (1853-1918), an independent, powerful, and essentially Swiss artist. In Hodler's time there were other significant developments. German-speaking Swiss artists, who had hitherto gone to Germany (preferably to Munich) to study, began to look to Paris for aesthetic leadership. Toward the end of the nineteenth century Félix Vallotton (1865-1925), a precocious artist from the canton of Vaud, joined the circle of the Nabis. Giovanni Giacometti (1868-1933), an Italian-speaking artist from the Grisons, was strongly influenced by Van Gogh.

When war broke out in 1914, there was a general exodus of Swiss artists working in Paris, and their eventual return to Switzerland gave a new impetus to the artists there, with impressive results. Among those who returned was René Auberjonois (1872-1957), a native of Vaud. After a long period of struggling with aesthetic problems of his time, he evolved a highly personal mature style; his later work was subtly poetic.

Alberto Giacometti (1901-1966), the sculptor, and a son of Giovanni Giacometti, was adept at drawing and painting. Early in the 1920's he moved to Paris, but he returned frequently to his home village of Stampa. He left hundreds of excellent examples of graphic art—drawings with an intense, nervous line made with a pointed, hard pencil.

More than one third of the drawings assembled here have been contributed by the Print Room of the Oeffentliche Kunstsammlung in Basel, which has never before lent such a large number of drawings. Thirty of these, including nearly all the drawings by Urs Graf, Niklaus Manuel Deutsch, Hans Holbein the Younger, and Ambrosius Holbein, come from the Amerbach Collection, whose history is worth recalling.

The deaths of Ambrosius Holbein (about 1519), Urs Graf (1527-28), Manuel (1530), and Hans Holbein the Younger (1543) occurred at a time of great spiritual upheaval. The Reformation and the social struggles which in many places led to peasant wars changed the intellectual climate of Europe. The Gothic style, which had been so characteristic of the northern countries, went out of fashion. It was supplanted by a new style based on classical antiquity. Because of this change the drawings left by Urs Graf and Manuel provoked little interest.

Holbein went to England in 1526 with only the barest necessities and perhaps a few portrait sketches as samples of his work. Most of his effects, including his designs for windows and for façade decorations, and his father's estate, he left behind in Basel. In London he preserved the drawings that he made for portraits and history paintings. He had to give up his final designs for goldsmiths' work, hence nearly all of these have been lost. All sketches and notations leading up to the finished drawings, however, remained in Holbein's possession, and after his death the bulk of this material was sent to his widow in Basel. Certain portrait sketches somehow became separated from this collection and these are in Windsor Castle today.

Holbein's workshop in Basel was taken over by the glass painters Balthasar Han and Maximilian Wischack, who from time to time used some of Holbein's window designs, which were still stored there.

In the latter half of the sixteenth century, as religious and social tensions lessened and life became more leisurely, princes, nobles, and later, other wealthy men began collecting valuable or unusual objects such as paintings, books, the work of goldsmiths, weapons, and samples of wood and rocks. This nostalgia for the past and the passion for collecting were directly responsible for the preservation of much that is valuable in art. Dürer's drawings thus went into the collection of Willibald Imhoff in Nuremberg, and subsequently to the Emperor Rudolf II, in Prague.

Basilius Amerbach (1533-1591), an avid collector, had inherited a great tradition. His grandfather Johannes (1430-1513), in the course of a long residence in Venice, had collected Italian woodcuts and engravings for use in his publishing business. Basilius' father Bonifacius (1495-1562), a law professor at the University of Basel, not only inherited these objects, but in 1536 he acquired the estate of Erasmus of Rotterdam. This estate included—in addition to books and letters—a number of paintings, drawings, and various other art objects which Erasmus had received as gifts. In his turn Basilius Amerbach inherited this collection and added over 4000 engravings and nearly 2000 drawings. The latter group contained the artistic legacies of Urs Graf, Niklaus Manuel Deutsch, and the three Holbeins, which for decades had remained intact. Thanks to Basilius Amerbach's zeal as a collector, these priceless works of art have been preserved for posterity. This collection fortunately remained in the possession of the family until 1662, when it was put up for sale in Amsterdam. The city council of Basel purchased it for the university library chiefly for the books it contained. The collection's drawings and engravings did not then arouse much interest. Thus has a major part of the work of the most important early Swiss artists remained intact in Basel throughout the centuries.

Walter Hugelshofer

Catalog

ANONYMOUS MASTER, BERN, ABOUT 1500

1*. *Design for an Armorial Window for the Merchants' Guild, known as the "Zunft zu Safran," in Bern*

Pen and ink with wash. 42.8 x 31 cm., 16⅞ x 12¼ in.

Bern, Historisches Museum. Wyss Collection.

An itinerant merchant, accompanied by an assistant who carries on his back a frame with bundles of merchandise, offers two peasants an assortment of wares which he carries in a basket. One of the peasants is testing a knife; the other has his purse out in readiness to pay. Below, in the left-hand corner, is a chip box. An escutcheon, on which two crossed staffs surmounted by fleurs-de-lis have been hastily sketched, occupies the center foreground. At the top of the picture, monkeys plunder the merchant's box and one of the baskets, in a parody of the actions of the men below (a mocking reference to human vanity; see H. W. Janson, *Apes and Ape Lore in the Middle Ages and the Renaissance.* [Warburg Institute Studies 20], 1952, p. 221, pl. 43).

The drawing was made so that the client could have an idea of how the completed window would look. In the second decade of the sixteenth century, a division of labor developed between the draftsman who made the design and the glass painter who executed it. We have to distinguish between the sketch, such as this one intended for the patron, and the working drawing for the guidance of the glass painter.

This is the only drawing by this artist; its lively narrative power reminds us of the work of the Housebook Master. It may be that it was drawn by Lukas Schwartz, active in Bern from 1498 to 1526 as a designer of glass paintings.

LUX ZEINER

Lux (Lukas) Zeiner, a glass painter active in Zurich between 1480 and 1513, was one of the best, most original, and prolific producers of small painted windows, and was largely responsible for their popularity. He was a craftsman who made his own designs.

2. *The Emperor Charlemagne, Seated on a Throne between St. Felix and St. Regula, Patron Saints of Zurich*

Pen and ink. 34 x 25.3 cm., 13⅜ x 10 in.

* Bibliographical references may be found on page 172.

Karlsruhe, Staatliche Kunsthalle.

The drawing shown here was for Zeiner's patron. Its style shows Netherlandish influence, introduced through the work of Schongauer. A circular drawing by Zeiner, showing a hunting motif in which there are still many elements of Gothic, is in the Print Room of the Eidgenössische Technische Hochschule in Zurich.

HANS FRIES

Hans Fries, from Fribourg in Uechtland (*circa* 1465–*circa* 1518), was a contemporary (and a fellow craftsman in Augsburg) of Hans Holbein the Elder, with whose work he seems to have been familiar. From 1487 to 1497 Fries worked in Basel, then once again in Fribourg, and from 1510 onward in Bern, where he influenced the style of Niklaus Manuel.

3. *The Virgin and Child in a Landscape*

> Pen and ink, heightened with white, on reddish-brown tinted paper.
> 25.5 x 19.7 cm., 10 x 7¾ in.
>
> Basel, Oeffentliche Kunstsammlung, Print Room. Inv. no. 1959. 103.

The drawing shown here may well have been inspired by similar pictures made on color-treated paper by Hans Baldung in Strasbourg. Apart from this picture, only two other drawings by Hans Fries are known, one in Basel and the other in Munich—a sad reminder of the many works of art which have been lost over the centuries, through changes in taste and through accidental destruction.

LUCERNE MASTER, 1511

4. *The Donor, Anna Mangold, Asking Intercession of St. Anne, Her Patron Saint*

> Pen and ink with wash. 26.2 x 20.5 cm., 10¼ x 8⅛ in. Dated 1511.
>
> Bern, Kunstmuseum.

This is a working drawing, with instructions to the glass painter concerning colors. The artist is identified as a painter of altarpieces in Lucerne. Anna Mangold was the second wife of the mayor of Lucerne, Jakob von Hertenstein, a man fond of ostentation, who in 1517 employed the twenty-year-old Hans Holbein the Younger to paint his late Gothic house inside and out in the new style (Figure 38).

In this drawing St. Anne is shown with the Virgin Mary and the Christ Child.

URS GRAF

Urs Graf, the son of a goldsmith, was born about 1485 in Solothurn. He grew up in a time of increasing prosperity, when the general mood was one of elation following the series of unprecedented victories over the powerful Duke of Burgundy—it was also a time of deep spiritual unrest. Like his father, Urs Graf became a goldsmith. In 1503 he went to Strasbourg for training, and four years later, to Zurich. In 1509 he settled in Basel. Two years later he was persuaded to hire himself out for the Pope's short-lived campaign against the French in Milan. From that time until his death (1527 or 1528), Graf was fascinated by the mercenaries, with their fantastic garb and their daredevil existence. He captured their world and the long-vanished world of our forefathers in a great number of drawings. Of these, about a hundred (more than one half of the total) remain together, in the Print Room in Basel; the rest are scattered among many collections.

In 1511 Graf married, and the following year he became a citizen of Basel. At this time he designed illustrations for the flourishing new book trade, made working drawings for painted windows and experimented with etching. In 1515 he again made a trip across the Alps to fight in the war then raging around Milan. Despite repeated brushes with the law, Graf received a commission from the city council of Basel to cut the dies for some new silver coins. When Graf was imprisoned—as a punishment for breaking the law which forbade enlistment in foreign wars, and for other misdemeanors—his comrades secured his release so that he might compete in the Schützenfest.

Graf's drawings constitute the most significant part of his oeuvre and account for his survival as an artist and for his appeal today to a world so very different from his own. These drawings (mostly done in pen and ink on white paper) differ greatly, in both style and content. Often they seem hastily and carelessly executed, with little graphic charm; and they may be undisciplined in form and insensitive in content. At other times, however, they are uncompromising and direct, giving us a profound and often frightening insight into contemporary warfare and its effects on morals and manners, the intellectual and spiritual state of the Confederacy, and the moral degeneracy of a great many people, especially the young who, through early involvement in warfare had become wild and undisciplined. Given this background, we can understand how the Swiss, under Zwingli's leadership, were ready for the Reformation.

Some of Graf's drawings seem to be pictorial accounts of the wars—accounts in which the artist appears to patronize those who did not take part. Other drawings are like private confessions, in which the artist grimly mocks at his own weaknesses and openly airs his sins. At times he recalls François Villon. In his best drawings, Urs Graf shows a high degree of artistic integrity and an unusually daring presentation. Although most of Graf's drawings bear his monogram, they were not made for sale but were purely the products of his need to create. In this they stand alone in their time. And knowing this, we understand why Graf seldom dealt with religious themes and why, when he did, his pictures are not convincing.

5. *The Standard Bearer of Unterwalden*

Pen and ink. 29.5 x 18.8 cm., 11⅝ x 7⅜ in. Signed and dated 1521.

Zurich, Eidgenössische Technische Hochschule, Print Collection. Depositum Gottfried Keller Foundation. Inv. no. 121.

The standard was the ultimate symbol of martial strength and was credited with magical powers. It was always entrusted to the bravest man, and soldiers fought to the death in its defense.

6. *Lakeside Village*

Pen and ink. 21.5 x 15.5 cm., 8½ x 6⅛ in. Signed and dated 1514. The signatures and date are disproportionately large and prominent.

Basel, Oeffentliche Kunstsammlung, Print Room. Amerbach Collection. Inv. no. U. X. 62.

Urs Graf's virtuosity and his sheer delight in drawing are apparent in this landscape, which was composed freely from memory and not taken from nature. It is interesting to note that the rare landscapes of both Graf and Niklaus Manuel are definitely northern in character, although both artists had spent time in Lombardy.

7. *The Flagellation of Christ*

Pen and ink over a very fine pencil sketch. 19 x 18.5 cm., 7½ x 7¼ in. Signed and dated 1520.

Basel, Oeffentliche Kunstsammlung, Print Room. Amerbach Collection. Inv. no. U. 10. 98.

This drawing was made on the eve of the Reformation, at a time when most of Europe was undergoing a general examination of conscience. Urs Graf, the hardened soldier, has transformed the deeply moving religious theme of the flagellation of Christ into a brutal beating by rough mercenaries. While the grim subject matter repels in part, it attracts at the same time through the genius of its concept. In order to fully appreciate Graf's art, we must realize that an apparently cursory drawing such as this was in fact made from a preliminary sketch and was worked out much more carefully than might appear at first.

8. *Young Girl in Elaborate Dress*

Pen and ink. 23.8 x 20 cm., 9⅜ x 7⅞ in. Signed and dated 1518.

Basel, Oeffentliche Kunstsammlung, Print Room. Amerbach Collection. Inv. no. 1927.111.

We know of no model for this carefully executed sketch, with its great charm of line. On the girl's curiously shaped hat, below the ear, is a winged M surmounted by a coronet—a symbol often encountered in Graf's work. It might indicate an intimate relationship between the artist and the person who perhaps inspired the picture.

9. *Strolling Couple, Seen from Behind*

Pen and ink. 18 x 15.2 cm., 7⅛ x 6 in. Signed and dated 1514.

Basel, Oeffentliche Kunstsammlung, Print Room. Amerbach Collection. Inv. no. U.X.57.

In this drawing the artist has captured his subject in a few powerful lines, creating a genre picture which hints at caricature. Such artistic license is unique for this time. The M surmounted by a coronet, in the lower right-hand corner, may have been an allusion to the woman. Though incomprehensible to us today, it may have had a special significance in Graf's circles.

10. *Lovers beside a Lake*

Pen and ink. 14.5 x 10.5 cm., 5¾ x 4⅛ in. Signed. In the lower left-hand corner is an unintelligible sign, presumably incomplete.

Basel, Oeffentliche Kunstsammlung, Print Room. Amerbach Collection. Inv. no. U.10.113.

About this time many artists, among them Dürer and Altdorfer, began to replace religious themes with worldly ones. Urs Graf's sketch of two lovers, though remarkably free (and even casual in appearance), captures the moment perfectly. The artist has had the good taste to carry his drawing no further. Also, he has kept his monogram to a size which fits in well with the composition.

11. *Council of War*

Pen and ink. 29 x 21.4 cm., 11⅜ x 8½ in. Signed and dated 1515.

Basel, Oeffentliche Kunstsammlung, Print Room. Amerbach Collection. Inv. no. 53a.

The highly independent Swiss troops sometimes changed sides in the course of a battle. Even in the thick of the fighting, the mercenaries might call a council to decide whom it was most profitable to fight. It seems incredible to us that men could appear on the battlefield in such fantastically befeathered headgear. It seems, however, that this bolstered their morale and helped intimidate the enemy. The rest of their costume, too, was worn more for effect than for comfort.

NIKLAUS MANUEL DEUTSCH

Niklaus Manuel Deutsch (1484-1530) came from a family of apothecaries and herbalists. His father, Emmanuel Alleman—whose name reveals his Germanic origin—had moved from Chieri, in Piedmont, to Bern. There, in 1460, he became a citizen and later a member of the city council, which assured his acceptance by the leading families of Bern. His son Niklaus changed his name from Alleman to Deutsch in 1509 when he married, and took a shortened form of his father's Christian name as his surname. In his signature he identifies himself proudly as Niklaus Manuel Deutsch of Bern.

The earliest works of Manuel go back to around 1510. His drawings were nearly always signed, but seldom dated. They show young soldiers dressed in the flamboyant new fashions. These tall youths wear close-fitting garments; on their heads are berets with long, sweeping plumes. One can hardly believe that this fantastic garb was the ideal attire for murderous man-to-man combat in a narrow alpine pass. The young soldier was the hero of the Swiss from about 1470 to 1530—a time during which one stirring victory followed upon another. Indeed, Manuel appended a short dagger to his monogram years before he ever used one in battle.

We have no details of his work up to 1510, nor do we know with whom he studied. It could have been with Hans Fries, from whom Manuel might have learned the technique of using colored paper. In any case, much of his success stemmed from his own great talent. Between 1512 and 1522 Manuel's output grew ever richer and more varied. He painted saints for altarpieces. His secular work included decorative panels painted with the classical subjects so popular during the Renaissance (Pyramus and Thisbe, the Judgment of Paris, etc.). Some 140 drawings, approximately 90 of which are in the Print Room of the Oeffentliche Kunstsammlung in Basel, give us a comprehensive view of the contemporary world of ideas. There are noticeably few religious subjects but a great many didactic ones, such as the Wise and Foolish Virgins (which Manuel had also used for a woodcut), the old man and the young wife, and the memento mori of the Dance of Death. These are largely studies of individuals rather than group scenes, and are executed in the most varied techniques. They reveal a man of tremendous vitality, with a strong feeling for harmony and beauty—an imaginative artist of markedly independent spirit. He maintains his objectivity throughout, and his artistic expression is always controlled.

Despite his great output (a large proportion of which survived the Reformation and its attendant iconoclasm), and despite the fact that he sat in the city council of Bern, Manuel did not earn enough to support himself and his family adequately. In 1516 and again in 1522 he secretly served as a scribe to the pro-French party in the campaign in Italy. Later he freely admitted that he had hoped to enrich himself with booty. Though his action brought him into disgrace with his superiors in the government, he asked for and was granted an official position—the governorship of Erlach, a high administrative post. At this point Manuel gave up painting, declared himself a partisan of the Reformation, and took to writing on its behalf. He served on diplomatic missions, and only in his last years did he occasionally return to his art. He lived to see the altars which he had painted ripped out of the churches and destroyed.

12. *The Virgin Mary, Seated, with the Infant Jesus*

Pen and ink, heightened with white, on brown tinted paper.
23.5 x 18.3 cm., 9¼ x 7¼ in.

Karlsruhe, Staatliche Kunsthalle.

This striking, carefully executed master drawing, which shows the Virgin Mary seated out-of-doors, with the Christ child resting His head on Her knee, is one of Manuel's few drawings having a religious theme.

13. *Nude Woman with Two Children*

Pen and ink, heightened with white. 30.2 x 19.5 cm., 11⅞ x 7¾ in. Signed.

Karlsruhe, Staatliche Kunsthalle.

In subject matter and in treatment this sketch reflects the world of the Renaissance and shows the artist to be an independent talent—in touch with his times and willing to break with the past. This fine master drawing to some extent recalls Hans Baldung.

14. *Death Comes for the Canon*

Pen and ink with wash, heightened with white, on brown tinted paper. 22.8 x 18.9 cm., 9 x 7½ in. Signed.

Darmstadt, Hessisches Landesmuseum.

Sometime between 1515 and 1517 Manuel painted a 48-panel Dance of Death, with life-size figures, on the wall of the Dominican monastery in Bern. Like its prototype, the famous Dance of Death in Basel, this skillful work indicates, with uncompromising force, that Death takes all ranks and spares none—a grim memento mori for an age in which almost ceaseless warfare and the ensuing pestilence took so many in the prime of life. The drawing in Darmstadt, which shows Death as an old woman blowing on a shawm, leading a canon away, is not a preliminary sketch for the mural but is a later drawing which for some particular reason Manuel wished to keep. The mural deteriorated within a few decades, but the drawing gives us a very good idea of its character and its merit.

15. *Young Woman, Drawn in Profile*

Black and colored chalks with watercolor. 23.8 x 19.3 cm., 9⅜ x 7⅝ in.

Basel, Oeffentliche Kunstsammlung, Print Room. Amerbach Collection. Inv. no. U. X. 10.

In this drawing Manuel provides an ideal profile of a young woman who is self-contained and proud in bearing. The study may have been made during Manuel's last term as Governor of Erlach.

16. *Allegory on Man's Mortality*

Pen and ink, heightened with white, on yellow-brown tinted paper. 26.4 x 16.7 cm., 10⅜ x 6⅝ in. Signed.

Basel, Oeffentliche Kunstsammlung, Print Room. Amerbach Collection. Inv. no. U. X. 6.

A nude woman, fantastically adorned with ribbons, chains, and plumes, is seated on a curious globular stool, and in this conveyance she floats over a river valley. She holds the skull of a mercenary in her left hand; in her right is an hourglass surmounted by a sundial. On her knee she supports an incense burner. There are mountains in the background and fortifications beside the river. The meaning of the allegory eludes us, and this may have been the case with the artist as well. The woman may in part represent a sorceress (basically an erotic symbol); or she may be Vanitas, an allegory on the transitory nature of man's existence. Dürer's engraving of Nemesis and Baldung's pictures of witches may have influenced this work. The border shows that the picture was intended as a complete composition, such as the *Bathsheba* (Figure 51) or the *Lucretia*, also in the Oeffentliche Kunstsammlung in Basel.

17. *Soldier and a Young Woman*

Pen and ink, drawn over a very fine sketch. 28.5 x 19.2 cm., 11¼ x 7½ in. Signed.

Basel, Oeffentliche Kunstsammlung, Print Room. Amerbach Collection. Inv. no. U. X. 17.

This sketch of a fashionable couple was made when the Swiss wars were at their height. Despite the extreme elegance of his attire—the rich decoration of his garments and the excessively long sweeping plume in his beret—the youth gives the impression of manly seriousness and energy. The young woman radiates feminine charm. A late Gothic element is evoked by the use of the decorative scroll at the top, with its enigmatic characters reminiscent of the devices on objects contained in the loot which had recently come to the Swiss via Burgundy.

18. *The Foolish Old Man*

Pen and ink, heightened with white, on reddish-brown tinted paper. 20.3 x 18.8 cm., 8 x 7⅜ in.

Basel, Oeffentliche Kunstsammlung, Print Room. Amerbach Collection. Inv. no. U. XVI. 42.

The drawing shows an old man whose money has got him a young wife. Behind them a young man and woman seem destined to remain apart, no doubt because of the young man's lack of a similar fortune. The decorative scroll above bears the letters NKAW, interpreted as: *Niemand kann alles wissen* (No one can know everything). At a somewhat later date Lucas Cranach painted similar moralizing pictures, which foreshadow the approaching Reformation.

19. *St. Christopher*

Pen and ink. 20.3 x 15.3 cm., 8 x 6 in.

Basel, Oeffentliche Kunstsammlung, Print Room. Amerbach Collection. Inv. no. U. 10. 21.

This interpretation of St. Christopher carrying the Christ Child across a river is one of the most beautiful drawings of the early Germanic school.

20. *Rocky Peninsula*

Pen and ink. 28.2 x 20.5 cm., 11⅛ x 8⅛ in. Signed.

Basel, Oeffentliche Kunstsammlung, Print Room. Amerbach Collection. Inv. no. U.S. 19.

In this picture the artist has taken the component parts from nature but has combined them so as to produce a fantasy. Dürer and Patenir indulged in similar flights of fancy. The drawing shown here is one of Manuel's rare landscapes.

21. *Young Soldier in a Landscape*

Pen and ink, drawn over a very fine sketch. 27.3 x 19.2 cm., 10¾ x 7½ in. Circa 1512.

Private collection. Originally in the Carl Feer collection.

The drawing shows a young Swiss soldier in battle dress. He wears a beret which is held in place by a chin strap. A large feather, from which a little bell dangles, is attached to the beret. His richly worked garments fit him tightly; his right trouser leg is torn off. In his right hand the youth holds a lance (which could be as much as five yards long), and in his left a parrying weapon. A short dagger, fastened to his waist, lies athwart his back. On a tree stump, facing the soldier, a small sundial serves as a memento mori: *Tempus fugit*.

HANS LEU

Hans Leu was born about 1490 in Zurich, the son of a well-known painter who worked in the tradition of Schongauer. After receiving his early training at home, Leu went to work with Dürer in Nuremberg. There he met Hans Baldung, to whom he was drawn as a person and as a fellow artist. Around 1513 Leu returned to Zurich, where he took over his father's studio. Here he painted altarpieces and murals for churches, made designs for woodcuts and executed a number of drawings, either for his own pleasure or as designs for windows. In the summer of 1519 Dürer visited him in Zurich. In 1531 Leu was killed in the religious wars, in which he supported the reformer Zwingli.

Leu broke with tradition and, under Baldung's influence, produced works of remarkable artistic quality. Unlike other Swiss artists of his time, Leu was not deeply involved with the life of the mercenaries; in fact, he never portrayed a soldier. His feeling is tender and poetic, and his approach is gentle. Hans Leu is at his happiest and most original when depicting the charm of the mountain landscape of his homeland. He was one of the earliest artists to respond to the romantic aspects of the mountains. Many of his drawings were once ascribed to Altdorfer, whom Leu sometimes recalls. In fact, there was probably never any direct contact between the two artists. Both were active at the same time, in similar circumstances, and they arrived at similar results.

22. *Landscape*

Pen and ink. 21.8 x 15.8 cm., 8⅝ x 6¼ in. Signed and dated 1513.

Zurich, Kunsthaus.

This view from a mountainside, looking down on a castle by a lake, is one of the earliest landscape drawings without figures, and testifies to a changing approach to nature.

23. *St. Sebastian*

Pen and ink. 21.2 x 15.2 cm., 8⅜ x 6 in. Signed with monogram and dated 1517.

Nuremberg, Germanisches National-Museum. Hz. 33. K. 562.

The figure of the saint is based on an early woodcut of Hans Baldung, which was from Dürer's studio and was formerly attributed to Dürer (Bartsch, vol. vii, p. 180, no. 22). Leu's interpretation transforms Baldung's dramatic and passionate concept of the theme into one of lyric sentiment. The landscape, which is Leu's own contribution, shifts the emphasis of the composition. A mood of serenity pervades the picture.

24. *The Virgin Sitting under a Tree, with the Christ Child*

Pen and ink. 20.2 x 15.3 cm., 8 x 6 in. Signed with monogram and dated 1517.

Basel, Oeffentliche Kunstsammlung, Print Room. Amerbach Collection. Inv. no. U. XVI. 38.

A happy relationship between figure and landscape is seen here. This is one of the last pictures of the Madonna to have been made in Zurich. A few years later the Reformation broke out in Switzerland, and religious art became unpopular.

25. *St. Ursula in a Landscape*

Pen and ink. 14.1 x 11.2 cm., 5½ x 4⅜ in. Signed with monogram and dated 1516. The upper left-hand corner is missing.

Zurich, Eidgenössische Technische Hochschule, Print Collection. Depositum Gottfried Keller Foundation.

This figure of the saint looks almost as if it might be a statue carved in wood.

MASTER H. F. OF 1517

So far it has not been possible to identify with any certainty the artist who signed
his drawings with the monogram HF. The fact that some of the drawings are in the
Amerbach Collection makes it appear probable that he was active in the neighbor-
hood of Basel. In those uncertain times many artists had only a brief period of activity. Often they were killed in the frequent and bloody wars; or they fell victim
to the ensuing epidemics. Some artists, driven to seek more profitable fields elsewhere, might stay for only a short while in one place. A painter might show a brilliant but transitory flash of genius. We must not forget, too, that many works of
art have been lost to us in the course of the centuries, so that we have few clues left
to guide our research. Some of the very scanty data that we have for the artist who
signed himself HF might be attributed to the painter Hans Franck, who lived in
Basel and who fought in the Battle of Novara in 1515 (as did Niklaus Manuel) and
died before 1522. These data are not, however, sufficient for identification.

26. *Marching Soldier with a Sword on His Shoulder*

Black chalk. 31 x 22 cm., 12¼ x 8⅝ in. Signed with the monogram HF and dated
1517.

Basel, Oeffentliche Kunstsammlung, Print Room. Amerbach Collection. Inv. no.
U. IX. 420.

For all its mastery of execution and its apparent seriousness, this drawing seems to
be a caricature of the outlandish dress of the mercenaries: the feather of the soldier's beret is excessively long; his sword is of gigantic proportions; his clothing is
covered with slashes and trimmings. The soldier's pose is ridiculously exaggerated.

27. *Fortune*

Black chalk. 31 x 22 cm., 12¼ x 8⅝ in.

Basel, Oeffentliche Kunstsammlung, Print Room. Amerbach Collection. Inv. no.
U. VIII. 108.

A young woman is balanced on a globe, holding a goblet as a prize in one hand and a rudder in the other. On the scroll above her is the motto, "Glück hilf!" [Help me, Fortune!] Apparently the ironic subject matter was taken from the world of the mercenaries, who without having Fortune on their side could not expect to return home unscathed and laden with booty. In this new era the soldier, in his moment of desperation, no longer sought protection of the Virgin or of his patron saint—he wooed instead the vague spirit of Fortune. The hastily sketched incomplete drawing is not signed, but it was obviously done by the artist who drew the soldier carrying the sword and signed it HF (figure 26).

HANS FUNK, BERN, ca. 1524

About 1524 a portrait painter who signed himself HF and whose work showed the influence of Holbein and Manuel, was active in Bern.

28. *Young Man, Drawn in Profile*

> Black and red chalk. 26.3 x 17.7 cm., 10⅜ x 7 in. Signed at the left with a partly cropped F, which might originally have been HF. Above this is a cropped inscription which dates from the early nineteenth century: "Hans Funck von Bern, Glasmaler."

> Munich, Graphische Sammlung. Inv. no. 71.

Master H. F. may have been the author of this drawing. Should this prove to be the case, we should disregard the nineteenth-century attribution which appears here in the upper left-hand corner.

29. *Design for an Armorial Window for Jacob Mey*

> Pen and ink with wash, heightened with color. 56.5 x 59.5 cm., 22¼ x 23½ in. Signed with the monogram HFG (Han Funk Glasmaler). Dated 1532.

> Zurich, Kunsthaus. Z. Inv. no. 1938. 38.

This drawing, with its flamboyant decorative elements, suggests a rather bumptious self-assurance on the part of the Swiss, who had recently won a number of important battles. Stylistically, this sketch owes much to Holbein and Manuel. What we see here is not the working drawing but the sketch for Jacob Mey, who commissioned the window.

HANS HOLBEIN THE YOUNGER

Hans Holbein the Younger was born in Augsburg about 1497 (the exact date of his birth has not been established), at a time of growing prosperity for that city. Through its trade connections with Italy, Augsburg had become a leading port of entry for the ideas of the Renaissance. Powerful merchants invested large sums in new business ventures. The Diet of the Holy Roman Empire (always a source of new political and intellectual ideas) favored Augsburg as a meeting place. An atmosphere of splendor and ostentation characterized the city.

Holbein's father, Hans the Elder, a successful and highly respected painter, had established a workshop in which altarpieces were made. In this period of affluence the workshop flourished, and its products were shipped as far as Frankfurt. At that time such a workshop was primarily a family enterprise, in which as many members as could do so took part. Hans the Elder's brother Sigmund and his uncle Hans Maier worked for him, as did his sons Ambrosius and Hans, even when they were still boys. By 1515, however, this enterprise had failed—for what reasons we are not certain—and the various members of the family left Augsburg. After an unsuccessful attempt to establish themselves in Constance, the family finally settled in Basel. By now the two young sons had become the heads of the workshop, while their father acted more in the capacity of assistant. The Holbein family never quite recovered from the blow which had driven them from Augsburg. It cast a shadow over the life and work of the precocious son Hans; and it probably partially explained his reserve toward his fellow man and the severe, remote, almost odd quality which characterizes his work.

Once settled in Basel, Hans the Younger embarked on an extremely active career. In Lucerne in 1517, when barely twenty years old, he decorated the mayor's new house, inside and out, with murals. For this project he adopted the new style of the Renaissance, which he employed with instinctive ease and confidence. Eyes accustomed to the angular Gothic style were now dazzled by a rich architecture in the classical tradition—an architecture of columns, rounded arches and coffered ceilings. In these large and roomy halls Holbein's painted figures appeared to move with an easy grace.

From 1519 to 1526 Holbein lived in Basel, where he painted portraits of the leading citizens and decorated the altarpieces which it was their custom to donate to churches. Here he also illustrated books and made designs for woodcuts; in these areas his work was much sought after by the printers, who were always eager to find new talent. Holbein's work also included numerous designs for windows. In time he developed an extremely personal style, which was greatly admired and imitated. Set beside Holbein's work, that of an artist such as Urs Graf seems highly subjective, undisciplined and expressive.

In 1520 Holbein married and became a citizen of Basel. Later he decorated the council chamber of the Basel town hall with appropriate murals. Holbein joined no military expeditions to Italy, remained aloof from the political and religious struggles which accompanied the Reformation, but he did form a friendship with the learned and sophisticated Erasmus of Rotterdam. It was through Erasmus that Holbein found a new field of employment in London. He went there in 1526 without his family. The move was dictated by necessity, as the Reformation had sharply curtailed his earning power in Switzerland. In London he was well received. He was soon appreciated by the scholars, and his popularity quickly spread to court circles. In 1528 Holbein was back in Basel, and in the following spring he witnessed the iconoclastic upheavals which resulted in the destruction of his altarpieces in the churches. During this period he painted the portrait of his wife and two sons, a picture that is without parallel in the northern art of its time. He completed his murals in the town hall and executed other mural commissions.

At this time, however, Basel had not enough to offer a painter of Holbein's stature. In 1532 he returned to London, again leaving his family in Basel, which must have been unsatisfactory for both. In London Holbein did a series of brilliant portraits of merchants and of members of the royal family, including Henry VIII, to whom he became court painter. He also made many designs for goldsmiths and armorers. In 1538 Holbein was reunited with his family in Basel, but his stay was brief. He returned to London and to his position as court painter. He died there in 1543, a victim of the plague.

Holbein was a latecomer to the great artistic flowering of Dürer's time in Germany. When Holbein's career had just begun, Dürer was already an artist of major achievements. The painful struggles of transition from the late Gothic to the Renaissance, and the process of assimilating the new forms of expression developed in Italy through the rediscovery of antiquity, were something Holbein never had to reckon with. From the very beginning he easily mastered the new style, with its optimism and its humanism. The strong tendency toward expressiveness that was so characteristic of the south German artists was alien to Holbein. Even in his innovations he remained within his self-imposed bounds. His imagination enabled him to conjure up, seemingly without effort, a wide range of forms, which he employed with equal ease. The even strokes of his pen neither thicken nor become thin and never break off abruptly. Like his father, many of whose workshop techniques he adopted and whose example he followed as a portraitist, Holbein used modes of expression which differed sharply from those of other German draftsmen. While others indicated shadows by means of crosshatching with the pen, Holbein achieved this effect by applying a delicate wash with his brush—a technique which may have originated with the Netherlandish artists. Landscapes appear in his work merely as a background or setting for his figures. He never painted a landscape for its own sake.

Holbein rarely signed his drawings. He thought of most of them not as finished works of art but as preliminary stages for various projects. They all have in common an extraordinary purity of composition and a flawless pen technique. A draftsman of phenomenal achievement, Holbein has an enigmatic fascination that is completely his own.

30. *The Virgin Seated between Two Columns, Suckling the Infant Jesus*

Pen and ink with wash, heightened with white, on blue-gray tinted paper. 21.2 x 14.8 cm., 8⅜ x 5⅞ in.

Basel, Oeffentliche Kunstsammlung, Print Room. Amerbach Collection. Inv. no. 1662. 130.

This drawing dates from about 1520.

31. *The Prodigal Son as a Swineherd*

Pen and ink with wash. 30.6 x 20.9 cm., 12 x 8¼ in.

Basel, Oeffentliche Kunstsammlung, Print Room. Amerbach Collection. Inv. no. 1662. 157.

This design for an armorial window was made about 1518, probably in Lucerne. The escutcheon in the lower part of the drawing has been left blank.

32. *St. Elizabeth of Thuringia Feeding a Sick Beggar*

Pen and ink with wash. 37.3 x 30.7 cm., 14¾ x 12⅛ in.

Basel, Oeffentliche Kunstsammlung, Print Room. Amerbach Collection. Inv. no. 1662. 147.

In this design for a window St. Elizabeth of Thuringia is shown giving food to a sick beggar. On her right a knight in armor makes his obeisance. Two putti, wearing helmets, hold blank escutcheons on which armorial bearings can be inscribed. Below is a large slab, which has also been left blank for an inscription. This drawing dates from about 1523.

33. *Mercenaries in Combat*

Brush and wash, over a preliminary pen sketch. 28.5 x 44.1 cm., 11¼ x 17⅜ in.

Basel, Oeffentliche Kunstsammlung, Print Room. Amerbach Collection. Inv. no. 1662. 140.

Holbein never took part in any of the Swiss wars (although as a citizen of Basel he was obligated to do so), and he had no direct knowledge of combat. At this time the subject of warfare occupied men's thoughts everywhere, and the drawing shown here, which was done in England, may have been made at the request of someone who wanted to know what hand-to-hand fighting was like. The drawing has apparently been trimmed off on either side.

34. *The Bat*

Brush and wash with watercolor lightly applied. 16.6 x 22.9 cm., 6½ x 9 in.

Basel, Oeffentliche Kunstsammlung, Print Room. Amerbach Collection. Inv. no. 1662. 162.

Holbein apparently made this drawing (circa 1525) for his own interest and enjoyment—as Dürer did with his illustration of a Walrus.

35. *Portrait of Sir Nicholas Carew*

Black and colored chalks. 55 x 38.6 cm., 21⅞ x 15¼ in.

Basel, Oeffentliche Kunstsammlung, Print Room. Amerbach Collection. Inv. no. 1662. 34

Carew was a favorite of Henry VIII. He became Master of the King's Horse and served in several diplomatic and military missions to France. He later fell into disfavor, and was beheaded in 1539. The painting made from this drawing is in the possession of the Duke of Buccleuch (see Ganz, *Holbein*, 1950, number 3).

36. *Portrait of Lady Mary Guildford*

Black and colored chalks. 55.2 x 38.8 cm., 21¾ x 15¼ in. Dated 1527.

Basel, Oeffentliche Kunstsammlung, Print Room. Amerbach Collection. Inv. no. 1662. 35.

This drawing was made in one sitting, through a pane of glass. Holbein subsequently painted the model's portrait from the drawing, without any further sittings and with the aid of the model's clothes (see K. T. Parker, *Holbein Drawings in Windsor Castle*, London 1947). The painting is now in the Museum of Fine Arts in St.

Louis, Missouri (see Ganz, *Holbein*, London 1950, numbers 78, 80). The companion piece to the drawing, a portrait of Sir Henry Guildford, Chancellor of the Exchequer to Henry VIII, is in Windsor Castle, as is the painting made from it.

37. *Design for a Table Centerpiece*

Pen and ink. 40 x 17.4 cm., 15¾ x 6⅞ in.

Basel, Oeffentliche Kunstsammlung, Print Room. Amerbach Collection. Inv. no. 1662. 165. 99.

In London, as in Basel, Holbein was closely associated with the goldsmiths, among them Hans von Antwerpen and Hans von Zürich. Among his many designs for them is this particularly fine working drawing for a table centerpiece.

38. *Leaina before the Judges*

Pen and ink with wash. 18 x 13.7 cm., 7⅛ x 5⅜ in.

Basel, Oeffentliche Kunstsammlung, Print Room. Amerbach Collection. Inv. no. 1662. 159.

In the foreground Leaina, standing before her judges in a lofty and spacious hall, bites off her tongue rather than betray her lover, Aristogeiton. The theme was suggested to Holbein in 1517, when he was living in Lucerne, by a humanist—perhaps Johannes Zimmerman, whose portrait Holbein had painted. As an example of the ultimate expression of loyalty, the picture embodies the spirit of the Renaissance. The treatment of the composition may have been influenced by mural paintings from northern Italy, such as those by Romanino. The drawing was a sketch for the decoration of Jakob von Hertenstein's house in Lucerne.

39. *Design for the Decoration of the Façade of the "Haus zum Tanz," Basel*

Pen and ink with wash. 53.4 x 36.8 cm., 21 x 14½ in.

Basel, Oeffentliche Kunstsammlung, Print Room. Amerbach Collection. Inv. no. 1662. 151.

The Gothic "Haus zum Tanz" in Basel, belonged to the goldsmith Angelrot, for whom Holbein sometimes made working drawings. The ingenious design, with its classical architectural element and bold use of illusionist perspective, was intended to make the narrow façade appear broader and to give the house the appearance of a Renaissance palace. Holbein's studies are our only record of this project, as the house is no longer standing.

40. *Christ before Pilate ("Ecce Homo")*

> Pen and ink with wash. 43 x 30.6 cm., 16⅞ x 12 in.

> Basel, Oeffentliche Kunstsammlung, Print Room. Amerbach Collection. Inv. no. 1662. 167.

This is one of an unfinished series of window designs of the Passion of Christ. The interpretation is Holbein's own. The dignified restraint of expression adds to the drawing's powerful effect. It is probable that Holbein prepared a number of such drawings to have on hand for potential patrons. The example shown here was made about 1525.

41. *Two Centaurs*

> Pen and ink with wash. 10.3 x 18.2 cm., 4⅛ x 7¼ in. Trimmed on all four sides. The lower left-hand corner is missing.

> Basel, Oeffentliche Kunstsammlung, Print Room. Amerbach Collection. Inv. no. 1662. 165. 53.

In this goldsmith's drawing, done about 1540 in London, Holbein has created a beautiful work which foreshadows the art of the seventeenth century.

42. *Design for a Goblet with a Lid*

> Pen and ink with wash and watercolor. 29.1 x 21.5 cm., 11½ x 8½ in.

> Basel, Oeffentliche Kunstsammlung, Print Room. Depositum Gottfried Keller Foundation. Inv. no. 629.

This detailed drawing was made for the patron, to give him a clear idea of how the finished object would look. A comparison of the design on this goblet with that on the doublet in Holbein's portrait of Henry VIII in the Rohoncz Castle Collection, Lugano (1948 catalogue, number 16), leads us to believe that the goblet may have been commissioned by the monarch. The shading on the lower right was added later.

AMBROSIUS HOLBEIN

Ambrosius Holbein (circa 1494–circa 1519) was the elder brother of Hans Holbein the Younger. He trained as a painter in his father's Augsburg workshop where, despite his youth, he was allowed to work side-by-side with the journeymen. In 1514 he went to Constance—whether to join a studio or to work independently, we do not know. By 1515 he was in Basel. In 1517 one Ambrosius Holbein, a painter from Augsburg, paid to join the painters' guild, called the "Zunft zum Himmel." He became a citizen of Basel in 1518.

Ambrosius designed book illustrations and ornaments for such enterprising printer-publishers as Froben, Petri, Cratander, and Gegenbach. These designs are delightfully imaginative, but, unfortunately, the blocks are not well cut. Like his brother, Ambrosius made designs for goldsmiths and armorers. He also painted some portraits and small altarpieces, which reveal the extent of his talent. In 1519 his career, which had begun so auspiciously, came to an abrupt end. We assume that he died in that year. His surviving works are proof that he had already moved far beyond the late Gothic traditions of his father's workshop, and had become a Renaissance artist. The work of this young painter seems to radiate a spirit of youth and reflect his cheerful nature and amiable character. Playful putti are a common motif in his work. Though as an artist he in some ways resembled his father and his brother, he had developed a definite style of his own in his brief lifetime.

43. *Portrait of a Young Man with a Cap*

Silverpoint and red chalk on paper with a white ground, with wash added (probably by the artist). 20.15 x 3 cm., 7⅞ x 6 in. Signed and dated 1517.

Basel, Oeffentliche Kunstsammlung, Print Room. Amerbach Collection. Inv. no. 1662. 207a.

The sitter was presumably one of Ambrosius' young friends—perhaps a fellow artist from the painters' guild, to which, in 1517, Ambrosius had applied for membership. The drawing is a finished portrait and not a study for a painting.

44. *Portrait of a Young Man with a Cap*

Silverpoint. 19.1 x 15.7 cm., 7½ x 6¼ in.

Basel, Oeffentliche Kunstsammlung, Print Room. Amerbach Collection. Inv. no. 1927. 110.

This handsome, skillfully executed drawing possesses all the hallmarks of a work by a member of the Holbein family. It is not easy to decide which of the three Holbeins was the author. While some have thought it might possibly be the work of the younger Hans, the general feeling is that the style is closer to that of Ambrosius.

JOST AMMAN

Jost Amman, the son of a scholar and teacher, was born in Zurich in 1539. He received his early training from glass painters. Through Dürer, Nuremberg had become the center of German art. Its artistic climate and economic situation were in many ways parallel to those of Zurich. It is not surprising, therefore, that Amman, when he came to Nuremberg in the course of his travels, chose to settle there, and as the successor to Virgil Solis soon became the leading craftsman in his field. He worked mainly as a designer of woodcuts. These designs were in great demand, particularly among the publishers in Frankfurt. While the work of his contemporary, Tobias Stimmer, is fresh and natural, that of Amman is labored and scholarly.

45. *Bacchus*

Pen and ink. 12 x 16 cm., 4¾ x 6¼ in. Signed and dated 1585.
Basel, Oeffentliche Kunstsammlung, Print Room. Inv. no. 1910. 22.

TOBIAS STIMMER

Tobias Stimmer was born in Schaffhausen in 1539. The spirit of optimism of the heroic early days of the confederation was only a memory when Stimmer's career began. The Reformation, with its austere and uncompromising outlook, had established itself in the larger towns of the country. Because the new religion had no need of paintings, the artist was limited to secular subjects, such as portraits, book illustration, and designs for various kinds of decorative work. The vigor and intensity of early Germanic art had vanished, and Northern artists now looked to Italy for inspiration. What attracted them most in Italian art was the decorative detail.

At a time when most Swiss artists seemed lost and without a sense of direction, Stimmer emerges as a vital figure and an extrovert. The latter is revealed most clearly in his portraits. In Schaffhausen Stimmer decorated the façade of a house with frescoes in the style of Holbein and the painters of northern Italy. He also made window designs for glass painters. In 1570 he moved to Strasbourg, then a flourishing city. There he was engaged chiefly in book illustration, but he also did some decorative paintings for the cathedral clock. From 1576 to 1579 he worked on murals for the great hall in the new castle of the Margrave of Baden-Baden, which is no longer standing. Stimmer died in Strasbourg in 1584.

46. *Deer Hunt on Horseback*

Pen and ink. 21.9 x 17 cm., 8⅝ x 6¾ in. Signed.

Zofingen, Stadtbibliothek.

In 1575 in Strasbourg Stimmer drew a series of hunting scenes—hunts for bear, boar, deer, and hare—for his friend the publisher Bernhard Jobin. They were to have been used for woodcuts illustrating a book on the hunt. The book was not completed, as Stimmer moved to Baden-Baden, but was published posthumously, with illustrations by Stimmer's students and fellow artists, Christoph Murer and Daniel Lindtmeyer. Today Stimmer's drawings for this work can be found in Munich, Bern, Zofingen, and Zurich.

47. *Squirrel*

Brush with watercolor. 22 x 14.5 cm., 8⅝ x 5¾ in. Signature added at a later date.

Zurich, Kunsthaus. Z. Inv. no. 1939/42.

Stimmer's straightforward rendition of nature strikes a refreshing note when compared with the Mannerist productions of his contemporaries.

48. *Self-Portrait*

Pen and ink with watercolor. 20 x 15.2 cm., 7⅞ x 6 in. Inscribed: "Tobias Stimer von Schaffhaussen."

Donaueschingen, Fürstlich-Fürstenbergische Collection.

Bendel's suggestion that this unusual portrait may be a self-portrait is now generally accepted. The inscription is ambiguous: it is probably both title and artist's signature, but it could be merely the latter.

49. *Courtroom Scene*

Pen and ink. 42.1 x 31.4 cm., 16¼ x 12⅜ in.

Zurich, Schweizerisches Landesmuseum. Inv. no. LM 25646.

In this design for a window only the main features appear, drawn with great clarity for the benefit of the glass painter. The scene in the upper part of the picture represents a boar hunt.

50. *The Three Graces: Aglaia, Euphrosyne, and Thalia*

> Brush, heightened with white, on gray ground paper. 18.5 x 16.6 cm., 7¼ x 6½ in. Signed. Below, in the center, the inscription "Gratie."

> Berlin, Staatliche Museen, Print Room. 2105.

In Greek mythology, the Graces, daughters of Zeus, were the personifications of beauty, charm, and grace.

DANIEL LINDTMEYER

Daniel Lindtmeyer was born in Schaffhausen in 1552. A precocious and highly gifted artist, he came early under the influence of Tobias Stimmer, for whom he worked at one time, in Strasbourg. A highly skilled draftsman whose work had an unusual beauty of line, Lindtmeyer experienced to the full the bitterness of trying to develop his talents and make a living as a painter in a Protestant country. His designs for the decorative arts show great imagination, particularly his drawings for glass painters, which in time found a wide market. His rather turbulent and unsettled life came to an end in 1604.

51. *David and Bathsheba*

> Pen and ink, heightened with white, on brown ground paper. 38.9 x 29 cm., 15⅜ x 11⅜ in. Signed and dated 1578.

> Basel, Oeffentliche Kunstsammlung, Print Room. Inv. no. 1956.92.

The drawing shows David watching Bathsheba as she bathes. Although this picture reminds us in many ways of the work of the German late Gothic artists, we see, on closer examination, that the lavish composition is in the opulent style of the German Renaissance. Our earlier impression, however, shows to what an extent the influence of the age of Dürer still lingered on as late as the second half of the sixteenth century.

52. *Children Dancing in a Row*

> Pen and ink with wash. 18 x 29.5 cm., 7⅛ x 11⅝ in. Inscribed "Da. L. M. v. S." [Daniel Lindtmeyer von Schaffhausen]. Dated 1597.

> Zurich, Eidgenössische Technische Hochschule, Print Collection. Depositum Gottfried Keller Foundation. Inv. no. 338.3.

53. *Scenes of Peasant Life*

Pen and ink with wash. 30.5 x 20.5 cm., 12 x 8⅛ in. Signed.

Zurich, Eidgenössische Technische Hochschule, Print Collection. Depositum Gottfried Keller Foundation. Inv. no. 338. 4.

These five scenes are designs for the upper portions of windows and were intended for the glass painter's use. They show the two chief occupations of the Swiss in earlier times—plowing and cheesemaking.

HANS HEINRICH WÄGMANN

Hans Heinrich Wägmann (Wegmann) was born in Zurich in 1557. He trained in Zurich and worked there for a time. After experiencing the difficulties of making a living as a painter in a Protestant state, he moved, in 1582, to Lucerne, which was a Catholic city. There he found ample employment as a painter of frescoes and altarpieces. A few sketches are the only remaining examples of his work.

54. *Girl Reading*

Pen and ink. 18.4 x 11.3 cm., 7¼ x 4½ in. Signed and dated 1595.

Basel, Oeffentliche Kunstsammlung, Print Room. Inv. no. 1963. 157.

This study of a girl reading is an unusual and particularly charming example of Wägmann's work.

JOSEPH WERNER

Joseph Werner, the son of a painter, was born in Bern in 1637. He trained first under Merian in Frankfurt; later, in 1654, he went to Rome, where he became a painter of miniatures. In this fashionable medium he painted portraits and numerous historical scenes and allegories. He worked in Paris for Louis XIV, and in Augsburg, Munich, and Innsbruck for the reigning princes. In 1682 Werner returned to Bern and remained there until 1695, when he became director of the newly created Academy in Berlin. He retired from this post in 1707 and died in 1710. In his drawings, which are completely different from his miniatures, Werner seems to have been influenced in his choice of theme by the fantasies of Salvator Rosa. The macabre world of witchcraft and magic of the Middle Ages, so dear to Hans Baldung, reappears here in a more romantic guise.

55. *Self-Portrait in His Studio, before an Easel*

Brush with wash, heightened with white. 25.5 x 19.9 cm., 10 x 7⅞ in. In the lower right-hand corner is the inscription: "Werner" (possibly added later).

Bern, Kunstmuseum. Inv. no. A 7219.

56. *Armida*

Brush with wash. 35 x 22.3 cm., 3¾ x 8¾ in. Signed: "J. Werner inv." Below is the inscription: "Armida."

Bern, Kunstmuseum. Inv. no. A 8421.

In Torquato Tasso's novel *Jerusalem Delivered*, Armida, the daughter of King Arbilan of Damascus, uses her beauty and her magic powers to lure the knight Rinaldo into her enchanted garden. She detains him there with sensual pleasures, to keep him from carrying out his mission to free Jerusalem from the infidel.

57. *The Witch of Endor Summoning the Ghost of Samuel*

Brush and wash, heightened with white. 35.2 x 32 cm., 13⅞ x 12⅝ in. Dated 1677.

Bern, Kunstmuseum. Inv. no. A 1196.

The subject is taken from Samuel I, chapter 28. The Witch of Endor summons the ghost of the prophet Samuel on behalf of the apprehensive Saul, who seeks advice in time of war.

JOHANNES DÜNZ

Johannes Dünz, the son of a painter, was born in Brugg in 1645. A good portrait painter, he moved to Bern, where he could more easily earn his livelihood. He was also a painter of landscapes and still lifes. He died in 1736.

58. *View of the Berner Oberland from the Hills near Bremgarten*

Pen and ink with watercolor. 28.5 x 60 cm., 11¼ x 23⅝ in. Signed and dated 1686 (on the back).

Zurich, Schweizerisches Landesmuseum. Inv. no. LM 25883.

This landscape shows the river Aar as it winds past the castle of Bremgarten, near Bern. At the far right is the squat tower of the cathedral; across the expanse of the middle distance is the Oberland, the group of the Eiger, Mönch, and Jungfrau. With its objective treatment of nature, reminiscent of the Dutch artists, this work anticipates the delicate landscapes of the Swiss painters of a hundred years later.

64. *Portrait of a Man*

Black chalk, heightened with white and red chalk, on blue paper. 56 x 44 cm., 22 x 17¼ in.

Geneva, Musée d'Art et d'Histoire. Gift of the Société des Amis du Musée. Inv. no. 1935.5.

The sketch was taken from life to be completed later in the studio, without the model. (Holbein often used this method for his paintings.) This drawing admirably conveys the force and vitality of Liotard's draftsmanship.

65. *A Woman in the Streets of Chios*

Red, black, and white chalk. 21 x 13 cm., 8¼ x 5⅛ in. Dated July, 1738, and inscribed by the artist "Femme Turque dans les rues."

Céligny, private collection.

Liotard made this drawing while on a trip through the Greek Islands accompanied by Mr. Posonby.

JEAN HUBER

Jean Huber, whose family came originally from the Tyrol, was born in 1721, into the aristocracy of Geneva. He chose a military career and led the life of an officer and gentleman, first in the service of the Landgrave of Hesse and later in that of the King of Sardinia. In 1752 he returned to Geneva, where he held public office and settled down as a man of birth and substance. Huber's drawings and paintings show him to have been a talented and witty dilettante. He is best known to us through his association with Voltaire during the latter's stay in Ferney, and for his honest and realistic portrait studies of this great philosopher and writer. Huber died in 1786.

66. *Three Portraits of Jean Jacques Rousseau, Viewed from Different Angles*

Chalk. Each 20.6 x 7.6 cm., 8⅛ x 3 in.

Zurich, Kunsthaus. Z. Inv. no. 1944/14.

The philosopher Jean Jacques Rousseau (1712–1778), who was born in Geneva, spent most of his adult life abroad. Huber and Rousseau must have met, however, either in Geneva or elsewhere, at which time these three portraits may have been done.

ANTON GRAFF

Anton Graff was born in Winterthur in 1736 and died in Dresden in 1813. He trained as a portrait painter in Winterthur and in Augsburg. In 1766 he became court painter in Dresden; he also worked in Leipzig and Berlin. In Goethe's time Graff was the most popular portrait painter in Germany. On rare occasions he returned for short visits to Winterthur, where he undertook a number of commissions. Graff's portraiture is esteemed for the artist's skill in delineating character and for the rapport he seems to have with his sitters.

67. *Self-Portrait*

> Chalk, heightened with white, on gray paper. 35 x 27.5 cm., 13¾ x 10⅞ in.
> Lucerne, Kunstmuseum.

68. *Portrait of a Man*

> Chalk, heightened with white, on brown paper. 40.8 x 27 cm., 16 x 10⅝ in.
> Zurich, Kunsthaus. Z. Inv. no. 1938/38.

SIGMUND FREUDENBERGER

Sigmund Freudenberger was born in Bern in 1745 and died there in 1801. He was a pupil of Handmann. From 1765 until 1773 he earned his living as a book illustrator in Paris, working for, and sometimes collaborating with, Boucher, Greuze, Roslin, and Aved. He designed the illustrated book *History of French Manners and Dress in the Eighteenth Century;* this project was later taken over by Moreau the Younger. The highly sophisticated and artistically stimulating atmosphere of Paris permanently influenced Freudenberger's style and approach. After his return to Bern he applied what he had learned to subject matter taken from peasant life.

69. *Harp Player*

> Red chalk. 23 x 17.7 cm., 9 x 7 in. Signed and dated 1778.
> Zurich, Schweizerisches Landesmuseum. Inv. no. 35864.

70. *Portrait of a Young Man*

> Pen with watercolor. 24 x 18.3 cm., 9½ x 7½ in.
> Zurich, Kunsthaus. Z. Inv. no. 1939/190.

77. *Dante and Vergil at the Entrance to the Underworld*

Pen and ink with pencil and wash. 49.5 x 64 cm., 19½ x 25⅛ in. Inscription and date: "Rome 1772."

Zurich, Kunsthaus. Z. Inv. no. 1938/766.

This drawing was inspired by Dante's *Divine Comedy*.

78. *Mamillius with a Lady-in-Waiting*

Pen and ink with watercolor. Diameter 49 cm., 19¼ in.

Zurich, Kunsthaus. Z. Inv. no. 1914/42.

This drawing is based on a scene in Shakespeare's *A Winter's Tale*. Act II, Scene 1.

79. *Lady of Fashion*

Pencil and watercolor. 31.5 x 23.5 cm., 13⅜ x 9½ in. Dated 1790.

Zurich, Kunsthaus. Z. Inv. no. 1914/32.

Füssli's unusual imagination can be seen in his inventive designs for feminine attire, which were well in advance of fashion. We do not know to what extent fashion took notice of his flights of fancy.

JOHANN JAKOB BIEDERMANN

Johann Jakob Biedermann was born in Winterthur in 1763 and died in Zurich in 1830. While still quite young he came to Bern, where, under the influence of Aberli, he developed into an excellent landscape painter. He was employed as landscape painter on the estates of the Bernese aristocracy, particularly that of the Vaud, which was then part of the canton of Bern. The French Revolution, with the resultant collapse of the aristocracy, had its effect also on the rising bourgeoisie of Bern, and Biedermann was forced to seek employment elsewhere. From 1814 to 1827 he lived in Constance. Biedermann, a keen observer and recorder of nature, was one of the earliest masters of Swiss landscape painting.

80. *Gentleman's Carriage before a Park Gate*

Brush and pen and ink with watercolor. 9.5 x 10.7 cm., 3¾ x 4¼ in.
Signed and dated 1797.

Zurich, Eidgenössische Technische Hochschule, Print Collection. Inv. no. 672s.

81. *View from the Great Terrace of the Chateau of Carrouge*

Pen and ink with watercolor. 52.8 x 80 cm., 20¾ x 31½ in. Signed and dated 1785. Bern, Historisches Museum. Inv. no. 1257.

The castle of Carrouge is near Moudon, above Lausanne.

WOLFGANG ADAM TÖPFFER

Wolfgang Adam Töpffer (1766–1847) was born in Geneva. He was trained in Paris, where his studies were interrupted by the French Revolution. A follower of De La Rive, he was an excellent landscape painter, whose work revealed a deep feeling for nature. By 1800 he had become one of the leading artists of the Geneva school and had much to do with the emergence of that city as an art center after a long unproductive period. Töpffer was a hard worker and a tireless student of nature. He had a lively imagination, a genial disposition and a delightful sense of humor. In his works, whether drawings, watercolors, or oil paintings, Geneva and its countryside and inhabitants appear in their most pleasing aspect. Töpffer's reputation spread beyond the borders of his own country; he was highly regarded in England and France.

82. *Seated Girl with Arms Crossed*

Pencil with white chalk, heightened with white, on blue paper, with intended colors indicated. 28.5 x 20.5 cm., 11¼ x 8⅛ in.

Zurich, Kunsthaus. Z. Inv. no. 1938/420.

83. *Seated Girl in Profile*

Pencil. 24.1 x 19.1 cm., 9½ x 7½ in.
Zurich, Kunsthaus. Z. Inv. no. 1938/807.

84. *Seated Girl, Side View*

Pencil with watercolor, heightened with white, on brown paper. 20.2 x 22.7 cm., 8 x 9⅞ in.

Zurich, Kunsthaus. Z. Inv. no. 1938/421.

85. *Picnic beside Lake Leman*

Pencil with watercolor (unfinished). 53.5 x 42.5 cm., 21⅛ x 16¾ in.

Geneva, Musée d'Art et d'Histoire. Depositum Gottfried Keller Foundation. Inv. no. 927b.

LUDWIG VOGEL

Ludwig Vogel was born in Zurich in 1788. While a student at the Vienna Academy, from 1808 to 1810, he was associated with Pforr and Overbeck, the leaders of the Nazarene group. In 1810 Vogel went to Rome with this group (known at that time as the *Lukasbrüder*), and came into contact with Cornelius, Koch, and Thorvaldsen. He returned home in 1813, during the Napoleonic wars. Vogel's main interest lay in painting episodes from Swiss history. He made many drawings for these carefully worked out compositions, and traveled around the countryside in search of inspiration. His work is characterized by a distinctive style and a fondness for lofty themes. Vogel died in Zurich in 1879.

86. *Valeria Castle, near Sion*

   Pencil with watercolor. 23.6 x 42.7 cm., 9¼ x 16¾ in.
   Zurich, Schweizerisches Landesmuseum. Inv. no. LM 27383.

ARNOLD BÖCKLIN

Arnold Böcklin was born in Basel in 1827 and died in Florence in 1901. In the course of prolonged studies in Düsseldorf, Paris, and Rome, he developed a highly individual style, which was received enthusiastically in some quarters and rejected vigorously in others. His landscapes appear to stem from a great depth of feeling, and the artist seems to have delighted in what he saw. His scenes are peopled with figures drawn from his classical background—Pan and the nymphs, the hunt of Diana, and bacchanals. In this he was as artless and natural as Rubens, whose work he had studied on his own in Antwerp, Paris, and Munich. He spent much time in Weimar, Munich, Basel, and Zurich but his spiritual home was classical Italy. Böcklin was first of all a painter, and drawing played only a limited role in his creative scheme. Nevertheless, his drawings reveal great skill, a fine sensitivity, and considerable vitality.

87. *Faun*

   Charcoal, heightened with white. 17.8 x 29.9 cm., 7 x 11¾ in. Signed and dated 1864.
   Basel, Oeffentliche Kunstsammlung, Print Room. Inv. no. 1931.

The drawing is a study for the painting *Faun Whistling to a Blackbird*.

88. *Hermit*

Pen and ink. 29.7 x 25.5 cm., 11 ¾ x 10 in.

Basel, Oeffentliche Kunstsammlung, Print Room. Inv. no. 1923.75.

This drawing is related to the painting *Hermit* of 1863, in the Schack Galerie, Munich.

89. *The Hunt of Diana*

Pen and ink. 24.5 x 41.2 cm., 9⅝ x 16¼ in.

Basel, Oeffentliche Kunstsammlung, Print Room. Inv. no. 1901.12.

In antiquity it was commonly believed that the hunt of Diana was an elemental force—creative as well as destructive.

The drawing is related to the painting *The Hunt of Diana* of 1862 in the Oeffentliche Kunstsammlung, Basel.

ALBERT ANKER

Albert Anker (1831–1910) was born in Ins, in the canton of Bern, the son of a veterinary surgeon. As a young man, Anker studied theology, but later went to Paris, where he studied with Gleyre and at the École des Beaux-Arts. He also studied and traveled in Italy. Until 1890 Anker spent winters in Paris, returning each summer to work at his father's home in Ins. Anker was a man of natural distinction and a cultivated artist whose painting developed in the Paris tradition. Possessed of an exquisite sense of color, he delighted in painting scenes of peasant life in the Bernese countryside.

90. *Portrait of a Boy, Eugen Oser*

Pencil. 22 x 17.7 cm., 8⅝ x 7 in. Inscribed and dated: "19. Juni 1878."
Arlesheim, Professor Arthur Stoll.

91. *Small Child in a High Chair*

Watercolor over a pencil sketch. 20.1 x 15.5 cm., 7⅞ x 6⅛ in.
Zurich, Kunsthaus. Z. Inv. no. 1938/288.

92. *Peasant Boy*

Pencil. 28 x 20.7 cm., 11 x 8⅛ in. Signed.

Zofingen, Stadtbibliothek.

FRANK BUCHSER

Frank Buchser (1828–1890) came from Feldbrunnen near Solothurn. A born artist and a man of robust temperament, he made up for his lack of formal education by independent study abroad. In time he became a popular painter. His strength lay in a strong feeling for color and bold, free brushwork. After visiting Spain, Morocco, and England he went to the United States in 1866. The recent Civil War had focused the world's attention on America, and Buchser conceived the romantic notion that he, as a representative of Switzerland—the oldest democracy—should go and salute the youngest democracy and honor it with an enormous painting (which, however, never materialized). The artist arrived in Washington with official introductions, and General Banks placed a large studio at his disposal. Buchser had planned a composition containing numerous portraits of the leading political and military figures, but all that he achieved was a group of (sometimes excellent) individual portraits, made as studies. The subjects included President Andrew Johnson; Secretary of State William H. Seward; Generals Banks, Sherman, and Lee; the poet William Cullen Bryant; and others who have never been identified. There were still other portraits which have since disappeared.

In addition to this project Buchser painted many scenes from Negro life in Virginia (*The Song of Mary Blaine*), made various studies in oils, and did a number of sketches of the Great Plains and the Great Lakes—areas which had not then been opened up to any great extent. His first journey—in the company of General Sherman—led him from Missouri through Denver and into the desert, then back via Omaha to Chicago and up to Niagara Falls. In 1867 Buchser was painting in Virginia. Especially interested in the Indians, he went in the summer of 1868 to Cleveland and Detroit, thence by boat across Lake Superior to Sault Sainte Marie, and on to Houghton, Michigan. Buchser remained in the United States until 1871, drawing and painting assiduously, and keeping a diary. The oil studies and pencil sketches not left behind in America he gave to the Basel Museum. Most of his finished paintings, however, are in the Solothurn Museum.

93. *Niagara Falls*

Pencil. 29.8 x 48.3 cm., 11¾ x 19 in. Inscribed and dated: "Niagara. 6 Oktober 1866."

Basel, Oeffentliche Kunstsammlung, Print Room. Inv. no. 1896.66.616.

94. *St. Mary's Rapids*

Pencil. 24.5 x 52.6 cm., 9⅝ x 20¾ in. Inscribed and dated: "Rapids of St. Mary, Canada Hudson's Bay Post. 15 August 1868."

Basel, Oeffentliche Kunstsammlung, Print Room. Inv. no. 1896.66.40.

95. *Chippewa Camp on the Rapids*

Pencil. 21.3 x 34.6 cm., 8⅜ x 13⅝ in. Inscribed and dated: "Chipawa Camp on the Rapid. 26 August 1868. Kleine rötlich gelbe Blümchen am Vordergrund [Small reddish-yellow flowers in the foreground]."

Basel, Oeffentliche Kunstsammlung, Print Room. Inv. no. 1896.66.653.

96. *Rivona Floods*

Pencil. 10.8 x 22 cm., 4¼ x 8⅝ in. Inscribed and dated: "Rivona Floods. 30 September 1870."

Basel, Oeffentliche Kunstsammlung, Print Room. Inv. no. 1896.66.676.

97. *Portrait of a Young Lady*

Pencil. 30.4 x 25.4 cm., 12 x 10 in.

Basel, Oeffentliche Kunstsammlung, Print Room. Inv. no. 1896.66.380.

The sitter was presumably Mrs. Frederick Seward, a daughter-in-law of Secretary of State William H. Seward (1801–1872). The drawing was probably made at Seward's home in Auburn, New York.

98. *Portrait of T. W. Herick*

Pencil. 30.6 x 23.9 cm., 12 x 9⅜ in. Signed. Inscribed and dated: "T. W. Herick Esq. from St. Mary, 3. September 1868."

Basel, Oeffentliche Kunstsammlung, Print Room. Inv. no. 1896.66.416.

Buchser began this drawing on the trip to the Canadian lakes.

116. *Landscape near Vercorin (Valais)*

Pen and india ink with wash. 26.5 x 42 cm., 10½ x 16½ in. Signed.
Winterthur, Kunstmuseum.

117. *Sleeping Woman*

Chalk. 31.5 x 47 cm., 12⅜ x 18½ in. Signed.

Zurich, Kunsthaus. Z. Inv. 1929-25.

The drawing is a study for the central figure in the painting *Sleeping Women*, dated 1928, which is in the Oeffentliche Kunstsammlung, in Basel (Depositum der Schweizerischen Eidgenossenschaft).

118. *Market at Carouge*

Gouache and watercolor on green paper. 31 x 29.5 cm., 12¼ x 11⅝ in.
Signed and dated 1906.

Geneva, Musée d'Art et d'Histoire.

LOUIS MOILLIET

Louis Moilliet was born in Bern in 1880. After many years of work, he finally found himself as an artist some time between 1909 and 1914, when he was associated with Paul Klee and August Macke. He went often to Tunisia and to southern Spain, and many of his subtle watercolors show his attempts to capture their sun-drenched colors. Moilliet was a superb watercolorist. So great was his technical ability that his enchanting paintings seem to have been created effortlessly. Moilliet died in 1962.

119. *Early Morning Mist in Majorca*

Watercolor. 23.5 x 31.8 cm., 9¼ x 12½ in. Dated 1926.
Private collection.

120. *Lucerne*

Watercolor. 31.5 x 42.4 cm., 12⅜ x 16¾ in. Signed and dated 1919.
Private collection.

121. *Salé, Morocco*

>Watercolor. 23.9 x 27.3 cm., 9⅜ x 10¾ in. Dated 1921.
>Private collection.

122. *Medenine, Tunisia*

>Watercolor. 23.6 x 27.8 cm., 9¼ x 11 in. Dated 1920.
>Private collection.

ALBERTO GIACOMETTI

Alberto Giacometti (1901-1966), born in Stampa, in Italian-speaking Switzerland, was the son of the painter Giovanni Giacometti. His artistic gifts were revealed at a very early age. From 1922 onward he lived and worked in Paris, without, however, losing touch with Stampa. He strove hard to find his own position within the current movements in the art world and became one of the most respected artists in Paris. Between 1929 and 1935 he exhibited with the Surrealists, but later he went back to work from nature. His human figures became unnaturally small and elongated. Giacometti was a sculptor as well as a painter, and at the same time was passionately fond of drawing. These drawings, which are of a rare intensity of expression and unusual spirituality, are an important part of his oeuvre.

123. *The Studio*

>Pencil. 49.5 x 32.5 cm., 19½ x 12¾ in. Signed and dated 1957.
>Zurich, Mrs. Nelly Bär.

124. *Room in the House at Stampa*

>Pencil. 50.2 x 33 cm., 19¾ x 13 in. Signed and dated 1958.
>Bern, Private collection.

125. *Portrait of E. W. Kornfeld*

>Pencil. 50 x 32 cm., 19¾ x 12⅝ in. Signed and dated 1959.
>Bern, Private collection.

126. *Interior with Apples*

>Pencil. 50 x 33 cm., 19¾ x 13 in. Signed and dated 1958.
>Basel, Mr. and Mrs. Franz Meyer.

Illustrations

I. ANONYMOUS MASTER, BERN, CA. 1500, *Design for a Window for a Merchant's Guild*

2. LUX ZEINER, *The Emperor Charlemagne*

3. HANS FRIES, *Madonna*

4. LUCERNE MASTER, 1511, *Anna Mangold Asking Intercession of St. Anne*

5. URS GRAF, *The Standard-Bearer of Unterwalden*

6. URS GRAF, *Lakeside Village*

7. URS GRAF, *The Flagellation*

8. URS GRAF, *Young Girl in Elaborate Dress*

9. URS GRAF, *Strolling Couple*

10. URS GRAF, *Lovers beside a Lake*

11. URS GRAF, *Council of War*

12. NIKLAUS MANUEL DEUTSCH, *The Virgin Mary with the Infant Jesus*

13. NIKLAUS MANUEL DEUTSCH, *Nude Woman with Two Children*

14. NIKLAUS MANUEL DEUTSCH, *Death Comes for the Canon*

15. NIKLAUS MANUEL DEUTSCH, *Young Woman Drawn in Profile*

16. NIKLAUS MANUEL DEUTSCH, *Allegory on Man's Mortality*

17. NIKLAUS MANUEL DEUTSCH, *Soldier and a Young Woman*

18. NIKLAUS MANUEL DEUTSCH, *The Foolish Old Man*

19. NIKLAUS MANUEL DEUTSCH, *St. Christopher*

20. NIKLAUS MANUEL DEUTSCH, *Rocky Peninsula*

21. NIKLAUS MANUEL DEUTSCH, *Young Soldier in a Landscape*

22. HANS LEU, *Landscape*

23. HANS LEU, *St. Sebastian*

24. HANS LEU, *The Virgin Sitting under a Tree, with the Christ Child*

25. HANS LEU, *St. Ursula in a Landscape*

26. MASTER H. F., *Marching Soldier*

27. MASTER H. F., *Fortune*

28. HANS FUNK, *Young Man, Drawn in Profile*

29. HANS FUNK, *Design for an Armorial Window*

30. HANS HOLBEIN THE YOUNGER, *The Virgin Suckling the Infant Jesus*

31. HANS HOLBEIN THE YOUNGER, *The Prodigal Son as a Swineherd*

32. HANS HOLBEIN THE YOUNGER, *St. Elizabeth of Thuringia*

33. HANS HOLBEIN THE YOUNGER, *Mercenaries in Combat*

34. HANS HOLBEIN THE YOUNGER, *The Bat*

35. HANS HOLBEIN THE YOUNGER, *Portrait of Sir Nicholas Carew*

36. HANS HOLBEIN THE YOUNGER, *Portrait of Lady Mary Guildford*

37. **HANS HOLBEIN THE YOUNGER,** *Design for a Table Centerpiece*

38. HANS HOLBEIN THE YOUNGER, *Leaina before the Judges*

39. HANS HOLBEIN THE YOUNGER, *Design for the "Haus zum Tanz"*

40. HANS HOLBEIN THE YOUNGER, *Christ before Pilate*

41. HANS HOLBEIN THE YOUNGER, *Two Centaurs*

42. HANS HOLBEIN THE YOUNGER, *Design for a Goblet*

43. AMBROSIUS HOLBEIN, *Portrait of a Young Man with a Cap*

44. AMBROSIUS HOLBEIN, *Portrait of a Young Man with a Cap*

45. JOST AMMAN, *Bacchus*

46. TOBIAS STIMMER, *Deer Hunt*

47. TOBIAS STIMMER, *Squirrel*

48. TOBIAS STIMMER, *Self-Portrait*

49. TOBIAS STIMMER, *Courtroom Scene*

50. TOBIAS STIMMER, *Three Graces*

51. DANIEL LINDTMEYER, *Bathsheba*

52. DANIEL LINDTMEYER, *Children Dancing in a Row*

53. DANIEL LINDTMEYER, *Scenes of Peasant Life*

54. HANS HEINRICH WÄGMANN, *Girl Reading*

55. JOSEPH WERNER, *Self-Portrait*

ARMIDA.

56. JOSEPH WERNER, *Armida*

57. JOSEPH WERNER, *The Witch of Endor*

Bey Braungarten, auf der Höhe gegen Oberland.
von J. Dünz. 1696.

58. JOHANNES DÜNZ, *View of the Berner Oberland*

Eine der förchterlichen Aussichten in der Nachbarschaft der Teufelsbrüke.

J. Rud. Schellenberg fec.

59. JOHANN RUDOLF SCHELLENBERG, *The Schöllenen Gorge*

60. JEAN ÉTIENNE LIOTARD, *Archduke Peter Leopold*

61. JEAN ÉTIENNE LIOTARD, *Archduchess Maria Karolina*

62. JEAN ÉTIENNE LIOTARD, *Lord Mount Stuart*

63. JEAN ÉTIENNE LIOTARD, *The Artist as an Old Man*

64. JEAN ÉTIENNE LIOTARD, *Portrait of a Man*

65. JEAN ÉTIENNE LIOTARD, *A Woman in the Streets of Chios*

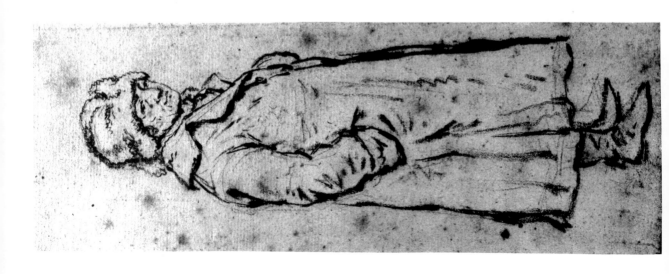

69. SIGMUND FREUDENBERGER, *Harp Player*

70. SIGMUND FREUDENBERGER, *Portrait of a Young Man*

71. LUDWIG ABERLI, *View of Erlach*

72. LUDWIG ABERLI, *Bremgarten Castle*

73. CASPAR WOLFF, *The Monastery of Engelberg*

74. CASPAR WOLFF, *Mountain Range*

75. CASPAR WOLFF, *Landscape*

76. JOHANN HEINRICH FÜSSLI, *Portrait of a Girl*

77. JOHANN HEINRICH FÜSSLI, *Dante and Vergil*

78. JOHANN HEINRICH FÜSSLI, *Mamillius with a Lady-in-Waiting*

Vue prise de la grande Terrasse du Chateau de Carrouge, en Juin 1785.

82. WOLFGANG TÖPFFER, *Seated Girl, Arms Crossed*

83. WOLFGANG TÖPFFER, *Seated Girl in Profile*

84. WOLFGANG TÖPFFER, *Seated Girl, Side View*

86. LUDWIG VOGEL, *Valeria Castle*

87. ARNOLD BÖCKLIN, *Faun*

above 88. ARNOLD BÖCKLIN, *Hermit*   *below* 89. ARNOLD BÖCKLIN, *The Hunt of Diana*

90. ALBERT ANKER, *Portrait of Eugene Oser*

91. ALBERT ANKER, *Child in a High Chair*

92. ALBERT ANKER, *Peasant Boy*

93. FRANK BUCHSER, *Niagara Falls*

94. FRANK BUCHSER, *St. Mary's Rapids*

95. FRANK BUCHSER, *Chippewa Camp*

96. FRANK BUCHSER, *Rivona Floods*

97. FRANK BUCHSER, *Portrait of a Young Lady*

98. FRANK BUCHSER, *Portrait of T. W. Herick*

99. FRANK BUCHSER, *Portrait of Captain Leith*

100. FERDINAND HODLER, *Portrait of a Young Girl*

101. FERDINAND HODLER, *Self-Portrait*

101a. FERDINAND HODLER, *Departure of the Jena Volunteers*   102. FERDINAND HODLER, *Study for "Empfindung"*

103. FERDINAND HODLER, *View of Mont Blanc*

104. FÉLIX VALLOTTON, *Still Life*

105. FÉLIX VALLOTTON, *Self-Portrait*

106. FÉLIX VALLOTTON, *Landscape near Fribourg*

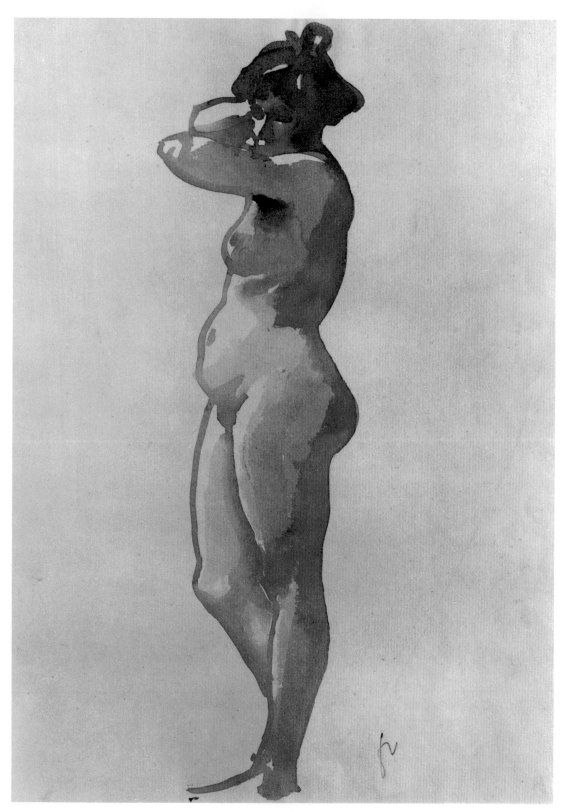

107. FÉLIX VALLOTTON, *Nude*

109. RENÉ AUBERJONOIS, *Acrobats*

108. RENÉ AUBERJONOIS, *Self-Portrait*

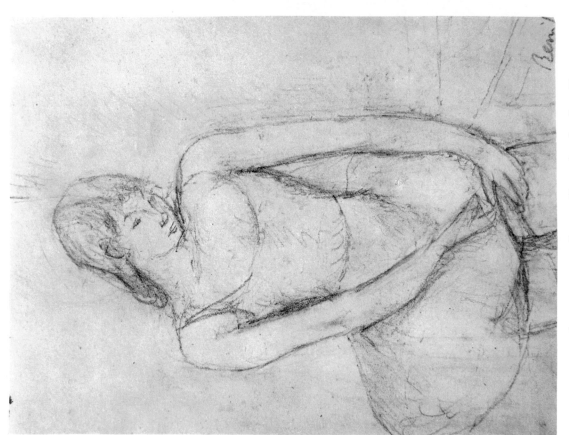

111. RENÉ AUBERJONOIS, *Dancer Fastening her Stocking*

110. RENÉ AUBERJONOIS, *Gathering the Grapes*

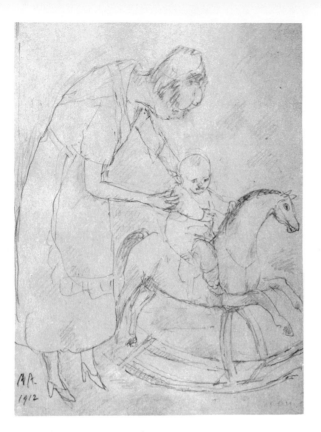

left
112. RENÉ AUBERJONOIS, *Mother and Child*

right
113. GIOVANNI GIACOMETTI, *Portrait of a Young Girl*

left
114. GIOVANNI GIACOMETTI, *Peasant Seated at Table*

below
115. GIOVANNI GIACOMETTI, *Shepherd Boy*

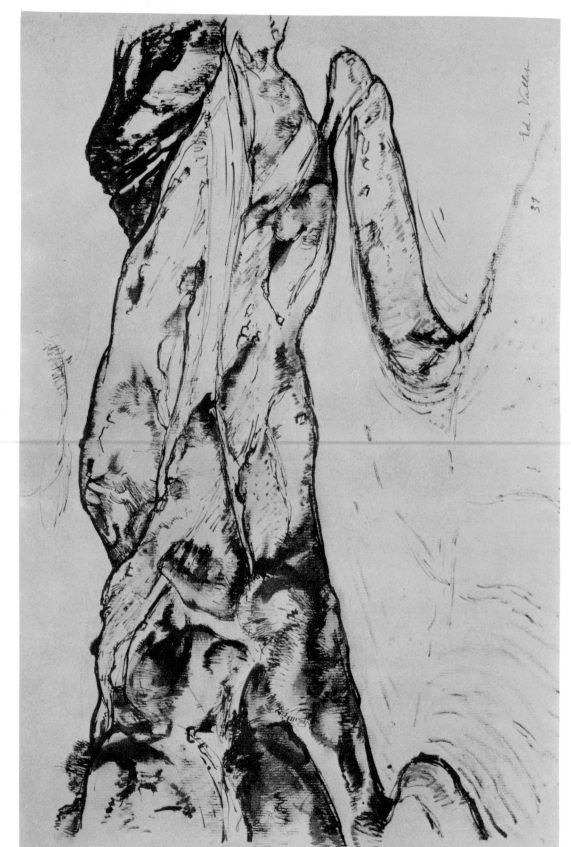

116. ÉDOUARD VALLET, *Landscape near Vercorin*

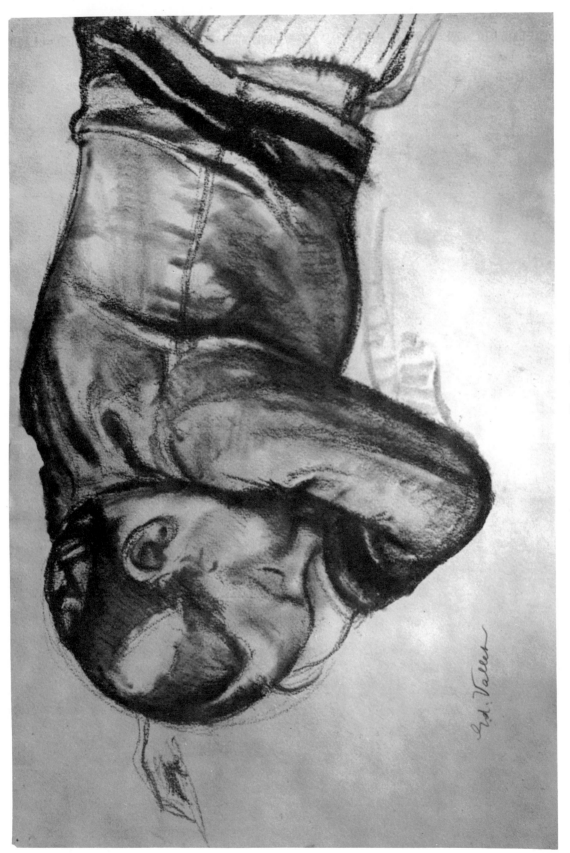

117. ÉDOUARD VALLET, *Sleeping Woman*

118. ÉDOUARD VALLET, *The Market at Carouge*

119. LOUIS MOILLIET, *Early Morning Mist in Majorca*

120. LOUIS MOILLIET, *Lucerne*

121. LOUIS MOILLIET, *Salé, Morocco*

122. LOUIS MOILLIET, *Medenine, Tunisia*

123. ALBERTO GIACOMETTI, *The Studio*

124. ALBERTO GIACOMETTI, *Room in the House at Stampa*

125. ALBERTO GIACOMETTI, *Portrait of E. W. Kornfeld*

126. ALBERTO GIACOMETTI, *Interior with Apples*

Abbreviations Used in References

ASAK	*Anzeiger für schweizerische Altertumskunde*
Baud-Bovy	Daniel Baud-Bovy, *Peintres genevois,* 1903
Bendel	Max Bendel, *Tobias Stimmer,* 1940
Die Malerfamilie Holbein	*Die Malerfamilie Holbein in Basel,* exhibition at the Kunstmuseum, Basel, during the 500th anniversary of the University of Basel, 1960
Ganz *Die Handzeichnungen Holbeins*	Paul Ganz, *Die Handzeichnungen Hans Holbeins des Jüngeren.* 1911-14, *Kritischer Katalog.* 1937.
Ganz *Handzeichnungen*	Paul Ganz, *Handzeichnungen schweizerischer Künstler des XV-XVIII. Jahrhunderts.* 3 volumes. 1904.
Hugelshofer *Die Meisterzeichnung*	Walter Hugelshofer, *Die Meisterzeichnung,* Volume I, "Schweizer Handzeichnungen des XV. und XVI. Jahrhunderts." 1928.
Koegler *Graf*	Hans Koegler, *Die Basler Handzeichnungen Urs Grafs.* 1926.
Koegler *Manuel*	Hans Koegler, *Die Basler Handzeichnungen des Niklaus Manuel Deutsch.* 1930.
Thöne	Friedrich Thöne, *Tobias Stimmer:* Handzeichnungen, 1936.

References

1. HANS LEHMANN, "Die Glasmalerei in Bern am Ende des 15. und Anfang des 16. Jahrhunderts." in *ASAK*, new series, volume XVI, 1913, page 206, and volume XVII, 1914, page 41. HANS LEHMANN, *Zur Geschichte der Glasmalerei in der Schweiz,* 1925, plate 19. WALTER HUGELSHOFER, *Die Meisterzeichnung,* volume I, "Schweizer Handzeichnungen des 15. und 16. Jahrhunderts," 1928, plate 7. HANS ROTT, *Quellen und Forschungen zur südwestdeutschen und schweizerischen Kunstgeschichte,* volume I, 1933-38, page 212, figure 81.

2. PAUL GANZ, Handzeichnungen schweizerischer Meister, 1908, volume I, plate 32. PAUL GANZ, *Malerei der Frührenaissance in der Schweiz,* 1924, page 107. HANS LEHMAN, 90. *Neujahrsblatt der Antiquarischen Gesellschaft Zürich,* 1925. HUGELSHOFER, *Die Meisterzeichnung,* plate 5. JENNY SCHNEIDER, *Die Standesscheiben von Lukas Zeiner im Tagsatzungssaal von Baden,* 1954.

3. JOSEPH MEDER, *Albertina Werk,* 1896, number 1048. HUGELSHOFER, *Die Meisterzeichnung,* plate 10.

4. LUCIE STUMM, "Niklaus Manuel, Hans Leu, und Hans Funk," in *ASAK*, new series, volume XI, 1909, page 247. WALTER HUGELSHOFER, *Festschrift für Robert Durrer,* 1927. HUGELSHOFER *Die Meisterzeichnung,* plate 40.

5. HANS KOEGLER, *Die Basler Handzeichnungen des Urs Graf,* 1926, number 136. W. LÜTHI, *Urs Graf und die Kunst der alten Schweizer,* 1928. MAX J. FRIEDLANDER and ELFRIED BOCK, *Handzeichnungen deutscher Meister des 15. und 16. Jahrhunderts,* no date.

6. KOEGLER *Graf,* number 49.

7. KOEGLER *Graf,* number 88.

8. KOEGLER *Graf,* number 81.

9. KOEGLER *Graf,* number 50.

10. KOEGLER *Graf,* number 18.

11. KOEGLER *Graf,* number 57.

12. DANIEL BURCKHARDT, in *Handzeichnungen schweizerischer Meister,* volume II, 1904-08, plate 22. HUGELSHOFER *Die Meisterzeichnung.* HANS KOEGLER, *Die Basler Handzeichnungen des Niklaus Manuel Deutsch,* 1930, number 3. C. VON MANDACH, H. KOEGLER, *Niklaus Manuel Deutsch,* 1940.

13. HUGELSHOFER *Die Meisterzeichnung,* plate 20. KOEGLER *Manuel,* number 108.

14. STUMM, in *ASAK*, 1909, page 253. HUGELSHOFER *Die Meisterzeichnung,* plate 16. KOEGLER *Manuel,* number 102. PAUL ZINSLI, *Der Berner Totentanz,* 1953.

15. GANZ *Handzeichnungen*, volume I, plate 51. KOEGLER *Manuel*, number 76.

16. KOEGLER *Manuel*, number 32.

17. KOEGLER *Manuel*, number 4.

18. KOEGLER *Manuel*, number 16.

19. KOEGLER *Manuel*, number 68.

20. KOEGLER *Manuel*, number 5.

22. WALTER HUGELSHOFER, "Das Werk des Zürcher Malers Hans Leu (I)," in *ASAK*, new series, volume XXV, 1923, page 167. WALTER HUGELSHOFER, *Die Zürcher Malerei bis zum Ausgang der Spätgotik*, 1928, page 47. WALTER HUGELSHOFER, "Hans Leu," THIEME-BECKER, *Künstlerlexikon*, 1929, page 142.

23. SCHÖNBRUNNER-MEDER, *Handzeichnungen alter Meister aus der Albertina und anderen Sammlungen*, 12 volumes, 1896-1908, number 1387. HUGELSHOFER, in *ASAK*, "Leu (II)," volume XXVI, page 33.

24. GANZ *Handzeichnungen*. HUGELSHOFER, in *ASAK*, "Leu (II)," volume XXVI, pages 28-42.

25. HUGELSHOFER, in ASAK, "Leu (I)," volume XXV, page 176; HUGELSHOFER, *Die Zürcher Malerei bis zum Ausgang der Spätgotik*, 1928.

26. HUGELSHOFER *Die Meisterzeichnung*, plate 38.

27. HUGELSHOFER *Die Meisterzeichnung*, plate 39.

28. HEINRICH ALFRED SCHMID, *Jahrbuch der preussischen Kunstsammlungen*, 1898, page 64. GANZ *Handzeichnungen*, volume I, plate 8. HUGELSHOFER *Die Meisterzeichnung*, plate 43. HALM, DEGENHART, and WEGENER, *Hundert Meisterzéichnungen*, 1958, plate 36.

29. STUMM, in *ASAK*, 1909, page 255. HUGELSHOFER *Die Meisterzeichnung*, plate 43.

30. A. WOLTMANN, *Hans Holbein und seine Zeit*, 2 volumes, 1863-76. PAUL GANZ, *Die Handzeichnungen Hans Holbeins des Jüngeren, Kritischer Katalog*, 1911-1937, number 107. W. WAETZOLDT, *H. Holbein d.J., Werk und Welt*, 1938. KARL THEODOR PARKER, *Die Zeichnungen Hans Holbeins in Windsor*, 1947. HEINRICH ALFRED SCHMID, *Hans Holbein der Jüngere*, 1948-1955. Catalogue of the exhibition, *Die Malerfamilie Holbein in Basel*, 1960, number 215.

31. GANZ *Die Handzeichnungen Holbeins*, number 199. *Die Malerfamilie Holbein*, number 202.

32. GANZ *Die Handzeichnungen Holbeins*, number 167. *Die Malerfamilie Holbein*, number 260.

33. GANZ *Die Handzeichnungen Holbeins*, number 125. *Die Malerfamilie Holbein*, number 317.

34. GANZ *Die Handzeichnungen Holbeins*, number 140. *Die Malerfamilie Holbein*, number 302.

35. GANZ *Die Handzeichnungen Holbeins*, number 33. *Die Malerfamilie Holbein*, number 307.

36. GANZ *Die Handzeichnungen Holbeins*, number 21. *Die Malerfamilie Holbein*, number 304.

37. GANZ *Die Handzeichnungen Holbeins*, number 219.

38. GANZ *Die Handzeichnungen Kritischer Katalog*, 1937, number 111. *Die Malerfamilie Holbein*, number 196.

39. GANZ *Die Handzeichnungen Holbeins*, number 114. *Die Malerfamilie Holbein*, number 269.

40. GANZ *Die Handzeichnungen Holbeins*, number 174. *Die Malerfamilie Holbein*, number 290.

41. GANZ *Die Handzeichnungen Holbeins*, number 252.

42. GANZ *Die Handzeichnungen Holbeins*, number 209.

43. *Die Malerfamilie Holbein*, number 95.

44. *Die Malerfamilie Holbein*, number 103.

45. KURT PILZ, *Die Zeichnungen des Jost Ammann*, 1933.

46. FRIEDRICH THÖNE, *Tobias Stimmer: Handzeichnungen*, 1936, number 97. MAX BENDEL, *Tobias Stimmer*, 1940, number 70.

47. THÖNE, number 21. BENDEL, number 22.

48. GANZ *Handzeichnungen*, volume III, number 57. MAX BENDEL, in *ASAK*, "Tobias Stimmer," 1926, page 119. THÖNE, number 57. BENDEL, number 20.

49. GANZ *Handzeichnungen*, volume I, plate 57. THÖNE, number 410.

50. THÖNE, number 26. BENDEL, number 103.

59. HEINZ KELLER, *Winterthurer Kleinmeister*, 1947.

60. FRIEDA BEERLI, *Die Kinder der Kaiserin*, undated, Insel-Büchlein number 613.

61. BEERLI.

63. FRANÇOIS FOSCA, *Liotard*, 1928, page 128.

64. DANIEL BAUD-BOVY, *Peintres genevois*, volume I, 1903, page 28.

66. BAUD-BOVY, volume I, page 45.

71. KELLER, page 13.

76. ARNOLD FEDERMANN, *Johann Heinrich Füssli*, 1927. PAUL GANZ, *Die Zeichnungen Hans Heinrich Füsslis*, 1947. NICOLAS POWELL, *The Drawings of Henry Fuseli*, 1951. FREDERICK ANTAL, *Fuseli: Studies*, 1956. GERT SCHIFF, *Zeichnungen von Johann Heinrich Füssli*, 1963.

82. BAUD-BOVY, volume I, page 19.

88. HEINRICH ALFRED SCHMID, *Arnold Böcklin, Handzeichnungen*, 1921, plate 22.

89. SCHMID, plate 28.

90. CONRAD VON MANDACH, *Albert Anker*, 1941. *Katalog der Sammlung Arthur Stoll*, 1961, plate 140.

93. H. LÜDEKE, *Frank Buchsers amerikanische Sendung 1866-1871*, 1941. GOTTFRIED WÄLCHLI, *Frank Buchser*, 1941. FRANK BUCHSER, *Mein Leben und Streben in Amerika*, edited by Gottfried Wälchli, 1942.

100. WALTER HUGELSHOFER, *Ferdinand Hodler*, 1952.

101a. *Katalog der Sammlung Arthur Stoll*, 1961, number 374.

104. HEDY HAHNLOSER, *Félix Vallotton et ses amis*, 1936. FRANCIS JOURDAIN, *Félix Vallotton*, 1953.

108. C. F. RAMUZ, *René Auberjonois*, 1943.

114. WALTER HUGELSHOFER, *Giovanni Giacometti*, 1936.

116. MARIA PICHEREAU, *Édouard Vallet*, 1934.

119. Article in: *Künstlerlexikon der Schweiz XX. Jahrhundert*, page 648. 1963.

123. ERNST SCHEIDEGGER, *Alberto Giacometti*, 1958. CHARLES DUPIN, *Alberto Giacometti*, 1962. *Katalog der Sammlung Werner und Nelly Bär*, 1965, plate 89.

Index of Artists